Developing an Assessment Framework for U.S. Air Force Building Partnerships Programs

Jennifer D. P. Moroney, Joe Hogler, Jefferson P. Marquis,
Christopher Paul, John E. Peters, Beth Grill

Prepared for the United States Air Force

PROJECT AIR FORCE

The research described in this report was sponsored by the United States
Air Force under Contract FA7014-06-C-0001. Further information may
be obtained from the Strategic Planning Division, Directorate of Plans,
Hq USAF.

Library of Congress Cataloging-in-Publication Data

Developing an assessment framework for U.S. Air Force building partnerships programs
  / Jennifer D.P. Moroney ... [et al.].
       p. cm.
    Includes bibliographical references.
    ISBN 978-0-8330-4738-0 (pbk. : alk. paper)
      1. United States. Air Force—Planning—Evaluation. 2. Military planning—
United States—Evaluation. 3. Military policy—International cooperation.
4. United States—Military relations—Foreign countries. I. Moroney,
Jennifer D. P., 1973–

U153.D48 2010
358.4'1356—dc22

                                                                      2009053632

Published 2010 by the RAND Corporation
1776 Main Street, P.O. Box 2138, Santa Monica, CA 90407-2138
1200 South Hayes Street, Arlington, VA 22202-5050
4570 Fifth Avenue, Suite 600, Pittsburgh, PA 15213-2665
RAND URL: http://www.rand.org/
To order RAND documents or to obtain additional information, contact
Distribution Services: Telephone: (310) 451-7002;
Fax: (310) 451-6915; Email: order@rand.org

Preface

The U.S. Air Force has a long history of working with allies and partners in a security cooperation context to build the defense capacities of these nations, acquire and maintain access to foreign territories for operational purposes, and strengthen relationships with partner air forces for mutual benefit. However, it is often difficult for the Air Force to evaluate whether or how these activities have contributed to the goals and objectives of U.S. national security, the Department of Defense (DoD), the combatant commands (COCOMs), and the services. As is the case throughout DoD, the Air Force currently does not have a comprehensive framework in place that will enable it to assess the effectiveness of its security cooperation efforts to support informed decisionmaking at many levels.

Despite a number of limitations, it is possible for the Air Force to conduct useful assessments that are consistent with guidance from the Secretary of Defense and that also provide the Air Force with valuable insights into the performance of the security cooperation programs for which it has responsibility. This monograph is intended to help the Air Force refine its approach by outlining an assessment framework that can allow Air Force planners, strategists, and key policymakers see specifically whether Air Force security cooperation programs and activities are achieving their intended effects.

This RAND Project AIR FORCE (PAF) monograph documents research performed for a fiscal year (FY) 2008 study "Developing an Assessment Framework for U.S. Air Force Security Cooperation." The work was sponsored by the Deputy Under Secretary of the Air Force for International Affairs (SAF/IA). It is the latest in a series of PAF documents supporting the Air Force's efforts to work with partner air forces in a spectrum of operations; it was conducted within PAF's Strategy and Doctrine Program.

Other PAF documents that address issues relating to security cooperation and building partnerships include the following:

- Jennifer D.P. Moroney, Kim Cragin, Eric Gons, Beth Grill, John E. Peters, and Rachel M. Swanger, *International Cooperation with Partner Air Forces*, MG-790-AF, 2009.
- Alan Vick, Adam Grissom, William Rosenau, Beth Grill, and Karl P. Mueller, *Air Power in the New Counterinsurgency Era: The Strategic Importance of USAF Advisory and Assistance Missions*, MG-509-AF, 2006.

RAND Project AIR FORCE

RAND Project AIR FORCE, a division of the RAND Corporation, is the U.S. Air Force's federally funded research and development center for studies and analyses. PAF provides the Air Force with independent analyses of policy alternatives affecting the development, employment, combat readiness, and support of current and future aerospace forces. Research is conducted in four programs: Force Modernization and Employment; Manpower, Personnel, and Training; Resource Management; and Strategy and Doctrine.

Additional information about PAF is available on our Web site: http://www.rand.org/paf/

Contents

Preface iii
Figures ix
Tables xi
Summary xiii
Acknowledgments xxi
Abbreviations xxiii

CHAPTER ONE
Introduction 1
The Air Force and Security Cooperation 3
   Defining Key Terms 3
   Understanding the Air Force's Security Cooperation Mission and
      Stakeholders 6
   Air Force Security Cooperation Program Objectives 7
   Key Security Cooperation Stakeholders 8
   Security Cooperation Guidance 10
Air Force and Security Cooperation Assessments 12
   Challenges to Assessing Air Force Security Cooperation Programs 13
Objectives and Key Research Questions 15
Research Design and Approach 16
Organization of the Monograph 16

CHAPTER TWO
The Key Elements of Air Force Security Cooperation 19
Guiding Expectations 19
Strategic Guidance 20

Global End States. 21
Combatant Command Regional or Functional End States. 22
Air Force Security Cooperation Goals 23
Air Force Security Cooperation Tools–"Ways" 25
Stakeholders. 27
State Department 28
DoD 28
Secretary of the Air Force. 28
Chief of Staff of the Air Force. 28
Combatant Commanders. 29
Deputy Under Secretary of the Air Force for International Affairs. 29
Deputy Chief of Staff for Air, Space, and Information Operations,
    Plans, and Requirements. 30
Air Component Commands. 30
Stakeholder Roles 32
Air Force Security Cooperation Programs 33
Authorities 35
U.S.C. Title 10 36
U.S.C. Title 22. 37
Air Force Governing Directives 39
Security Cooperation Resources. 41
Conclusions. 43

CHAPTER THREE
Principles of Assessment for Security Cooperation 45
What Is Assessment?. 45
Why Assess?. 46
Principles of Assessment and Evaluation Research. 47
Connecting Evaluation Research and Security Cooperation 48
Stakeholders Versus Assessment Stakeholders 48
Challenges to Security Cooperation Assessment. 49
The Hierarchy of Evaluation. 55
Level 1: Assessment of Need for the Program 55
Level 2: Assessment of Design and Theory 57
Level 3: Assessment of Process and Implementation 58
Level 4: Assessment of Outcomes or Effects. 59

Level 5: Assessment of Cost-Effectiveness 59
Hierarchy, Nesting, and Feedback 60
Generic Security Cooperation Assessment Questions and Data
    Requirements 61
Getting the Measures Right 62
Conclusions 67

CHAPTER FOUR
Illustrating the Assessment Framework 69
Approach 69
Program Descriptions 71
    Air Force Operator-to-Operator Staff Talks 72
    Chairman of the Joint Chiefs of Staff Exercise FLEXIBLE
        RESPONSE 73
    Canadian C-17 Foreign Military Sales Equipment Transfer and
        Training Case 73
Linking the Programs to the Levels of the Assessment Hierarchy 75
    Level 1: Assessment of Need for the Program 75
    Level 2: Design and Theory 79
    Level 3: Process and Implementation 85
    Level 4: Outcomes and Effects 94
    Level 5: Cost-Effectiveness 97
Conclusions 100

CHAPTER FIVE
Implementing a Comprehensive Assessment Framework 105
Assessment Options 105
Implementing Security Cooperation Assessments 108
    Title 10 Security Cooperation Programs Managed by the Air Force ... 110
    Title 10 Security Cooperation Programs Not Managed by the
        Air Force 110
    Title 22 Security Assistance Programs 111
    Assessment Functions 111
Air Force Assessment Organizations 112
Proposed Organizational Assignments and Criteria for Selecting
    Stakeholder Roles 113

Assessment Roles for Air Force–Managed Programs.................... 114
Assessment Roles for Other DoD-Managed Programs................... 118
Assessment Roles for Security Assistance Programs 119
Training for Assessments.. 121
A Proposed Air Force Assessment Approach.............................. 122
Conclusions.. 123

CHAPTER SIX
Conclusions and Recommendations 125
Conclusions.. 125
Recommendations 126
    Guidance... 126
    Assessment Management.. 127
    Assessment Activities 128
    Training.. 129

APPENDIXES
A. **Air Force Security Cooperation Programs (Illustrative)** 131
B. **Background on Case Studies** 141
C. **Assessment Examples** 163

Bibliography 173

Figures

S.1.   The Hierarchy of Evaluation.. xv
2.1.   Air Force Security Cooperation Supports Higher Goals........ 21
3.1.   The Hierarchy of Evaluation...................................... 56
5.1.   Implementing an Air Force Assessment Framework.......... 123

Tables

S.1. Summary of Programs, Stakeholders, and Assessment
Levels... xvii
1.1. Distinguishing the Term... 7
3.1. Generic Security Cooperation Assessment Questions and
Supporting Data 63
4.1. Case Studies, by Security Cooperation Way and Program
Category 71
4.2. Stakeholders and Needs Assessment Questions..................76
4.3. Stakeholders and Assessment Questions for Design and
Theory of a Program 81
4.4. Stakeholders and Assessment Questions for Process and
Implementation 86
4.5. Stakeholders and Questions for Assessing Outcomes and
Effects 94
4.6. Cost-Effectiveness Assessment Questions....................... 98
4.7. Summary of Programs, Stakeholders, and Assessment
Levels... 101
5.1. Responsibility-Assessment-Decision Relationships 107
5.2. Potential Assessment Roles for Air Force–Managed
Programs.. 115
5.3. Assessment Roles for Other DoD-Managed Programs 118
5.4. Assessment Roles for Security Assistance Programs.......... 120
A.1. Air Force Security Cooperation Programs..................... 131
B.1. Case Studies, by Security Cooperation Way and Program
Category 142

Summary

Introduction

The U.S. Air Force has a long history of working with allies and partners in a security cooperation context to build the defense capacities of these nations, acquire and maintain access to foreign territories for operational purposes, and strengthen relationships with partner air forces for mutual benefit. However, it is often difficult to determine whether or how these activities have contributed to the goals and objectives of U.S. national security, DoD, COCOMs, and the services. As is the case throughout DoD, the Air Force currently does not have a comprehensive framework in place by which it can assess the effectiveness of its security cooperation efforts with partner air forces in a deliberate and consistent way.

This monograph outlines an assessment framework that can enhance the Air Force's security cooperation efforts in a way that reflects U.S. national security interests, DoD guidance, COCOM requirements, and Air Force global priorities. The document identifies relevant Air Force security cooperation authorities, programs, and key stakeholders for those programs. The proposed assessment framework will allow Air Force planners, strategists, and key policymakers to see specifically whether Air Force security cooperation programs and activities are achieving the desired effects as defined in the guidance documents.

Principles of Assessment for Security Cooperation

Assessment is research or analysis to inform decisionmaking. When most people think of evaluation or assessment, they tend to think of outcomes assessment: Does the subject of the assessment "work"? Is it worthwhile? Although this is certainly within the purview of assessment, assessments cover a much broader range and can be quite varied. Assessment is fundamentally action-oriented. Assessments are conducted to determine the value, worth, or effect of a policy, program, proposal, practice, design, or service with a view toward making decisions about changing that program or program element in the future.

In short, the overall goal of assessment should remain the same: *Air Force security cooperation assessments should explicitly connect to Air Force decisionmaking.* Effective assessment and evaluation can be critical tools for informed decisionmaking and policymaking. Conversely, mismatched assessments can be worse than useless.

Air Force security cooperation assessment activities face a handful of additional challenges that must be overcome, worked around, or otherwise dealt with to achieve full success. These challenges include

- difficulty in determining causality or linking the activities of specific security cooperation programs to specific advances toward specific end states or outcomes
- paucity of well-articulated intermediate goals
- different assessment capabilities among Air Force stakeholders
- multiplicity of and differing priorities of stakeholders—a single organization can have different "stakes" as a stakeholder in different programs
- security cooperation data tracking systems not organized for security cooperation assessment
- confusing security cooperation terminology
- prevalence of delegating assessment responsibility to subordinate organizations
- expectations and preconceived notions of assessments.

The Hierarchy of Evaluation

Given the explicit focus on assessment for decisionmaking and the need to connect stakeholders and their decisionmaking needs with specific types of assessments, the Air Force needs a unifying framework to facilitate that matching process. That framework, grounded on "the hierarchy of evaluation,"[1] is presented in Figure S.1.

Level 1: Assessment of Need for the Program. Level 1, at the bottom of the hierarchy and foundational in many respects, is the assessment of the need for the program or activity. This is where evaluation connects most explicitly with target ends or goals. Evaluation at this level focuses on the problem to be solved or goal to be met, the

Figure S.1
The Hierarchy of Evaluation

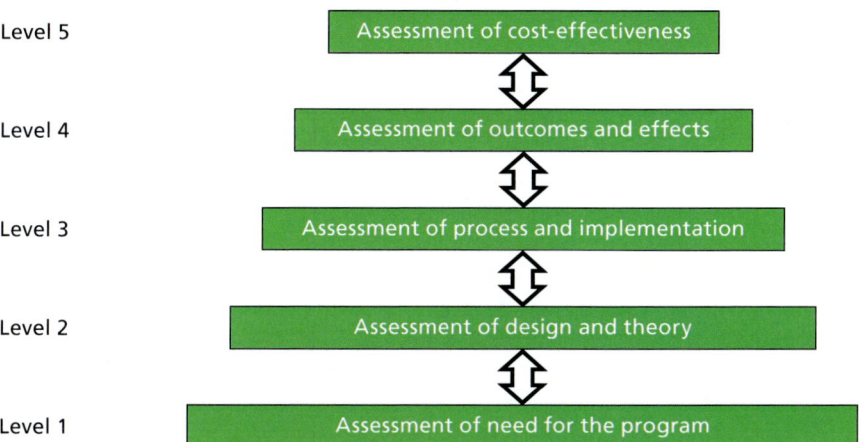

SOURCE: Adapted from Christopher Paul, Harry J. Thie, Elaine Reardon, Deanna Weber Prine, and Laurence Smallman, *Implementing and Evaluating an Innovative Approach to Simulation Training Acquisitions*, Santa Monica, Calif.: RAND Corporation, MG-442-OSD, 2006, Figure 7.1.
RAND *MG868-S.1*

---

[1]   See Peter H. Rossi, Mark W. Lipsey, and Howard E. Freeman, *Evaluation: A Systematic Approach,* Thousand Oaks, Calif.: Sage Publications, 7th ed., 2004.

population to be served, and the kinds of services that might contribute to a solution.[2]

Level 2: Assessment of Design and Theory. Assessment of the concept, design, and theory is the second level in the hierarchy. Once a needs assessment establishes that there is a problem or policy goal to pursue as well as the intended objectives of such policy, different solutions can be considered. This is where theory connects ways to ends.

Level 3: Assessment of Process and Implementation. Level 3 in the hierarchy of evaluation focuses on program operations and the execution of the elements prescribed by the theory and design at Level 2. A program can be perfectly executed but still not achieve its goals if the design was inadequate. Conversely, poor execution can foil the most brilliant design.

Level 4: Assessment of Outcomes and Effects. Level 4 is near the top of the evaluation hierarchy and concerns outcomes and effects. At this level, outputs are translated into outcomes, a level of performance, or achievement. Put another way, *outputs* are the products of program activities, *outcomes* are the changes resulting from the projects. This is the first level of assessment at which solutions to the problem that originally motivated the program can be seen.

Level 5: Assessment of Cost-Effectiveness. The assessment of cost-effectiveness sits at the top of the evaluation hierarchy, at Level 5. Only when desired outcomes are at least partially observed can efforts be made to assess their cost-effectiveness. Evaluations at this level are often most attractive in bottom-line terms, but they depend heavily on lower levels of evaluation.

The hierarchy of evaluation can be a powerful tool for appropriately matching types of assessment with specific stakeholder needs. Each level of the evaluation hierarchy implies a set of generic security cooperation assessment questions, the answers to which will differ considerably depending on the program's nature, the authorities of the stakeholders, and so forth.

Table S.1 summarizes the research team's analysis of the programs, the stakeholders, and the levels in which they are involved.

---

[2]   Rossi, Lipsey, and Freeman, 2004, p. 76.

Table S.1
Summary of Programs, Stakeholders, and Assessment Levels

| | Level of Analysis | | | | |
	Needs Assessment	Design and Theory	Process and Implementation	Outcomes and Effects	Cost-Effectiveness
Operator-to-Operator Staff Talks					
AF/CV					
AF/A3/5		√	√	√	√
SAF/IA		√			
HQ AF/A5XX	√	√	√	√	
Air Staff		√			
Components		√			
CJCS Exercise FLEXIBLE RESPONSE					
USAFE	√	√	√	√	
3 AF/CV	√				
3 AF/A9	√	√	√	√	
3 AF/A3XJ		√	√		
86 AW		√	√		
31 FW		√	√		
Canadian C-17 FMS Support Case					
SAF/IA	√	√	√	√	
HQ AMC		√	√	√	√
AFSAC	√	√	√	√	√
516 AESG	√	√	√	√	
HQ AF/A3OT			√		
HQ AETC/IA		√		√	√
AFSAT		√	√	√	
HQ AETC/A3		√			
19 AF		√			
373 TRS		√	√		

For the first four levels of analysis, stakeholders were conducting activities that could serve as sources of information to answer some of the generic assessment questions. However, as the table indicates, gaps remain, especially in the areas of needs and cost-effectiveness.

Implementing a Comprehensive Assessment Framework

All programs have stakeholders, and they each are guided by specific program authorities. Their authorities, which shape and influence their responsibilities, lead each stakeholder to a certain set of decisions they may make about the program:

- whether it should continue
- whether it is well-conceived given the theory of how the program is supposed to help the Air Force, or other stakeholders, reach their respective goals and end states
- whether the process and implementation of the program is performing adequately or requires revision
- whether the outcomes and effects of the program are meeting expectations
- whether the program is performing on a cost-benefit basis—delivering the expected "bang for the buck."

The Air Force plays roles in three general categories of security cooperation programs, each of which requires that the Air Force assume different roles for assessment purposes. First, for programs entirely under the Air Force's authority, assessments across the entire hierarchy of evaluation are possible. The key is to remember that the Air Force should assess only where it has decisions to make about the program.

Second, for Title 10 programs not managed by the Air Force, the Air Force faces no decisions with regard to the need for the program or the quality of its design and theory. Thus, Air Force involvement is likely to center on assessment of the process and implementation (e.g., are we following instructions?) and on outcome (e.g., what percentage of participants graduated from a course?).

Last, Title 22 security assistance programs also can be subject to the full scope of assessments. But again, the Air Force's role will be limited because other stakeholders have the authority to make the high-level decisions about the need for the program and the fit of its design and theory.

Recommendations

The Air Force should incorporate an assessment process at the program level into its current security cooperation assessment process to meet the Office of the Secretary of Defense (OSD) and Air Force needs. Second, it is important that Air Force stakeholders assess security cooperation with the intent to inform decisionmaking. Third, because of the limited assessment guidance and the need for efficient assessment processes, the Air Force should clarify and specify stakeholder assessment roles and responsibilities for security cooperation assessments.

Specific recommendations for implementing the assessment framework include the following:

Guidance

- SAF/IA should work closely with OSD to clarify program assessment responsibilities in the Guidance for Employment of the Force. (See p. 126.)
- SAF/IA should include an annex on assessments in the Air Force Global Partnership Strategy. (See pp. 126–127.)
- SAF/IA should consider assigning the responsibilities for data collection, assessment, assessment review, and assessment integration to stakeholders. (See pp. 111–123.)

Assessment Management

- Leverage assessment capacity and processes within the Air Force where they already exist. (See pp. 102, 127.)

- Emphasize security cooperation assessments as a focus area for the next annual SAF/IA global partnerships conference. (See pp. 127–128.)
- Ensure that SAF/IA is the assessment integrator, responsible for integrating service assessments with outcome-oriented assessments developed by the COCOMs, for programs involving the Air Force, rather than collecting data on specific programs and activities. (See pp. 117, 128.)
- Consider creating an Air Force Corporate Structure panel, chaired by SAF/IA, devoted to the security cooperation mission. (See pp. 102–103, 117–118, 128.)

Assessment Activities

- Consider a time-phased approach to data collection in which standardized assessment questions are asked to compare and contrast the results. (See p. 128.)
- Ensure that stakeholder objectivity is maintained in the program assessment framework. (See pp. 113, 129.)
- Knowledgebase should be the repository for programmatic assessments.[3] (See pp. 53, 129.)

Training

- SAF/IA should consider working with the Air Force's Institute of Technology's Center for Operational Analysis, Air University, Air Education and Training Command, and the Defense Security Cooperation Agency to develop a professional curriculum for security cooperation assessments. (See p. 129.)

---

[3] Knowledgebase is a centralized, useful repository of security coooperation data and guidance managed by SAF/IA.

Acknowledgments

The authors wish to thank a number of people for their support of the research reported in this monograph. First, our study sponsors, Col Kimerlee Conner and Mark Hoffman, members of the SAF/IA Strategy and Long Range Planning Directorate, provided excellent feedback and research assistance during the course of the year-long study. We are also grateful for the insightful discussions we had with officials from the following agencies: SAF/IA regional and functional desk officers; Headquarters AF/A3/5; Headquarters AETC/International Affairs; Air Force Security Assistance Training Squadron; Air Force Security Assistance Center; Air Force Central Command, Central Command; Pacific Air Forces, Pacific Command; Air Forces Southern Command, Southern Command; U.S. Air Forces South; Special Operations Command Europe, European Command; Special Operations Command Pacific; U.S. Army Security Assistance Command; U.S. Army Security Assistance Training Management Office; Inter-American Air Forces Academy; U.S. Marine Corps Headquarters; U.S. Coast Guard; U.S. Navy International Programs Office; 6th Special Operations Squadron; the National Guard 162nd Fighter Wing; and the Air Attaché community.

We greatly appreciate the thoughtful feedback provided by our RAND reviewer, Wade Markel, and our external reviewer, Lt Gen (Ret.) Jeffrey Kohler, now with the Boeing Company.

We also wish to acknowledge the contributions of numerous PAF research staff for their feedback on earlier briefings. We also very much appreciate the careful review of Michael Neumann, our communications analyst, and the help of our administrative assistant, Angela Cobbs.

Abbreviations

162 OG/CCI	162nd Operations Group, Regional Program Management Office
3 AF	Third Air Force
3 AF/A3XJ	Third Air Force Joint Exercise Branch
3 AF/A9	Third Air Force Directorate for Operational Analysis
3 AF/CV	Third Air Force Vice Chief of Staff
474 OG/PEP	474th Operations Group Personnel Exchange Program, Regional Program Management Office
AALPS	Automated Air Load Planning System report
ACC/A3TS	Air Combat Command Security Assistance Branch
AESG	Aeronautical Systems Group
AETC	Air Education and Training Command
AETC/A2/A3	Air Education and Training Command, Directorate of Intelligence and Air, Space and Information Operations
AETC/A3	Air Education and Training Command, Space and Information Operations
AETC/IA	Air Education and Training Command, International Affairs

AETC/IAD	Air Education and Training Command Foreign Disclosure Office
AFAA	Air Force Audit Agency
AF/A3/5	Air Force Deputy Chief of Staff, Operations, Plans, and Requirements
AF/A3OT	Air Force Operations Training Division
AF/A5X	Air Staff Directorate of Regional Plans and Requirements
AF/A5XS	Air Staff Concepts, Strategy, and Wargaming Division
AF/A5XX	Air Force Regional Plans and Issues Division
AF/A8	Air Force Strategic Plans and Programs Directorate
AF/A9	Air Force Studies and Analyses, Assessments, and Lessons Learned Directorate
AF/A9AO	Air Force Analysis and Assessments Division
AFCS	Air Force corporate structure
AF/CV	Air Force Vice Chief of Staff
AFELM/PEP	Air Force Elements Personnel Exchange Program
AFGPS	Air Force Global Partnership Strategy
AFI	Air Force Instruction
AFIT	Air Force Institute of Technology
AFM	Air Force Manual
AFMC	Air Force Materiel Command
AFPD	Air Force Policy Directive
AFSAC	Air Force Security Assistance Center
AFSAC/IAS	international affairs specialist
AFSAT	Air Force Security Assistance Training Squadron

AFSCS	Air Force Security Cooperation Strategy
AFSOC	Air Force Special Operations Command
AFSOC/A2S	Air Force Special Operations Command, Special Security Management
AFSPC/A8IF	Air Force Space Command Foreign Disclosure Branch
AMC	Air Mobility Command
AMW	air mobility wing
ANG	Air National Guard
AOR	area of responsibility
APPG	Annual Planning and Program Guidance
AW	airlift wing
BPC	building partner capacity
CENTCOM	U.S. Central Command
CJCS	Chairman of the Joint Chiefs of Staff
CJCSI	Chairman of the Joint Chiefs of Staff Instruction
CJCSM	Chairman of the Joint Chiefs of Staff Manual
COCOM	combatant command
COMSEC	communications security
CONUS	continental United States
CPX	command post exercise
CRDTE&P	Cooperative Research, Development, Testing, Evaluation, and Production
CSAF	Chief of Staff of the Air Force
CSBM	confidence and security building measure
CTFP	Combating Terrorism Fellowship Program
DCS	direct commercial sales

DISAM	Defense Institute of Security Assistance Management
DoD	Department of Defense
DoDD	Department of Defense Directive
DoDI	Department of Defense Instruction
DOS	Department of State
DSCA	Defense Security Cooperation Agency
EUCOM	U.S. European Command
FAA	Federal Aviation Agency
FMF	foreign military financing
FMS	foreign military sales
FSA	Freedom Support Act
FW	fighter wing
FY	fiscal year
GEF	Guidance for Employment of the Force
GSP	Globemaster III Sustainment Partnership
GTA	General Transfer Authority
HQ	headquarters
IAAFA	Inter-American Air Forces Academy
IAC	international armaments cooperation
IAS	International Affairs Specialist
IEP	Information Exchange Program
IG	inspector general
IMET	international military education and training
IMSO	International Student Management Office
IPR	interim progress review
IPT	integrated product team
ISR	intelligence, surveillance, and reconnaissance

LATAM Coop	Latin American cooperation
LOA	letter of offer and acceptance
MAJCOM	major command
MID	Management Initiative Decision
MOD	Ministry of Defence
MPEP	Military Personnel Exchange Program
NATO	North Atlantic Treaty Organization
NGB/SPP	National Guard Bureau State Partnership Program
O&M	operations and maintenance
OG	operations group
OJT	on-the-job training
ops-to-ops	operator-to-operator
ORF	official representation funds
OSD	Office of the Secretary of Defense
OSD/P	Office of the Secretary of Defense for Policy
PACAF	Pacific Air Forces
PACAF/XP	Pacific Air Forces Director of Plans
PACOM	U.S. Pacific Command
PAF	Project AIR FORCE
PEM	program element monitor
PL	Public Law
PMO	program management office/officer
PPBE	planning, programming, budgeting, and execution
QDR	Quadrennial Defense Review
R&D	research and development
RDT&E	research, development, test, and evaluation

ROI	return on investment
SAF	Secretary of the Air Force
SAF/FM	Office of the Assistant Secretary of the Air Force for Financial Management and Comptroller
SAF/IA	Office of the Deputy Under Secretary of the Air Force for International Affairs
SAF/IAPA	Office of the Deputy Under Secretary of the Air Force for International Affairs, International Airmen Division
SAF/USA	Deputy Under Secretary of the Air Force for Space Acquisition
SAO	Security Assistance Organization
SATCOM	satellite communications
SCG	Security Cooperation Guidance
SOUTHCOM	U.S. Southern Command
SPO	system program office
TCA	traditional combatant command activity
TRS	training squadron
TSCMIS	Theater Security Cooperation Management Information System
USAF	U.S. Air Force
USAFA/DFIP	U.S. Air Force Academy Office of International Programs
USAFE	U.S. Air Forces in Europe
USAFE/A3X	United States Air Forces in Europe Exercise Division
USAFE/A3XJ	United States Air Forces in Europe Joint Exercise Branch
U.S.C.	U.S. Code

WGS	wideband global SATCOM
WIF	Warsaw Initiative Fund
WMD	weapons of mass destruction
WSOC	Wideband Satellite Operations Center

CHAPTER ONE

Introduction

The U.S. Air Force has a long history of working with allies and partners in a security cooperation context to build the defense capacity of those nations, maintain and acquire access to foreign territories for operational purposes, and strengthen relationships with partner air forces for mutual benefit. The Air Force and other Department of Defense (DoD) entities conduct a host of activities with partner air forces, including training, equipping, and exercising, as well as other less-tangible activities, such as holding bilateral staff talks, workshops, and conferences, and providing educational opportunities.

However, it is often difficult to determine how, why, or if these activities have contributed to the goals and objectives of U.S. national security, DoD, the combatant commands (COCOMs), and the services. The Air Force, much like the other services, COCOMs, and DoD agencies, lacks an established framework by which it can comprehensively assess the effectiveness of its security cooperation efforts with partner air forces.

First, security cooperation assessments are necessary to support informed decisionmaking at many levels. For the services, assessments are useful to leaders who have to make decisions about existing programs, compare them, improve them, or possibly initiate new programs when assessments help identify gaps in current programs.

Programs are a logical unit of analysis for security cooperation assessments, largely because of the services' supporting role to the geographic COCOMs in the security cooperation arena.[1] The Office of the Secretary of Defense (OSD) in its guidance documents, specifically, the Guidance for Employment of the Force (GEF), requires that the services annually assess *program outputs*[2] for security cooperation.

Most Air Force security cooperation planners and implementers will say that they know intuitively, almost instinctively, whether they have made progress with their respective partner nations as a result of their individual activities. They often assert that the air force–to–air force relationship is "better" than it was before the activity. Although their intuition may be correct, it is very difficult to empirically demonstrate and validate what is only a general feeling of accomplishment.

Skeptics of security cooperation assessment efforts will often assert that the outcomes of these activities are not measurable, because the volume of activities with partner countries confounds anyone's ability to establish causality. In other words, they believe that it is impossible to attribute specific effects in the partner country either to individual, or collections of, programs or to activities that have a common goal.

However, in this monograph, we argue that despite these limitations, it is possible to conduct useful assessments that are consistent with the intent of the GEF and that also provide the Air Force with valuable insights into the performance of the security cooperation programs for which it has responsibility. Time-series assessment data, accrued over months or perhaps a few years, should reveal trends in programs that most observers would view as logically consistent with the health of the partner country relationship: improving, stable, or deteriorating. The key to finding these trends lies in the soundness of the assessment framework employed.

This monograph is intended to help the Air Force refine its approach to assessing the effectiveness of its security cooperation programs and activities around the world. In particular, it outlines an assessment framework that can enhance the Air Force's security coop-

---

[1] However, Air Force organizations may also engage in country, regional, needs, capabilities, and other types of assessments.

[2] "Outputs" are discussed throughout this monograph, but generally they are thought of as the products of program activities.

eration efforts and, specifically, its ability to work with partner air forces in a way that reflects U.S. national security interests, OSD guidance, COCOM requirements, and Air Force global priorities as described in the Air Force Global Partnership Strategy (AFGPS). The monograph identifies relevant Air Force security cooperation authorities, programs, and key stakeholders for those programs. The assessment framework will allow Air Force planners, strategists, and key policymakers to see specifically whether Air Force security cooperation programs and activities are achieving the desired effects as defined in the guidance documents.

The Air Force and Security Cooperation

Defining Key Terms

Two terms that are used throughout this monograph require explanation. *Security cooperation* and its subset *security assistance* are concepts with a long history of use. According to the Defense Security Cooperation Agency (DSCA) Web site, security cooperation includes

> those activities conducted with allies and friendly nations to: build relationships that promote specified U.S. interests, build allied and friendly nation capabilities for self-defense and coalition operations, [and] provide U.S. forces with peacetime and contingency access.[3]

Examples include training and combined exercises, operational meetings, contacts and exchanges, security assistance, medical and engineering team engagements, cooperative development, acquisition and technical interchanges, and scientific and technology collaboration.[4]

Security assistance is a subset of security cooperation and consists of "a group of programs, authorized by law that allows the transfer of

---

[3] See Defense Security Cooperation Agency, "Frequently Asked Questions," April 29, 2009.

[4] U.S. Air Force, Office of the Secretary of the Air Force for International Affairs, *Air Force Security Cooperation Strategy*, September 11, 2006b, p. 3.

military articles and services to friendly foreign governments."[5] Examples of these programs include foreign military sales (FMS), foreign military financing (FMF), international military education and training (IMET), and direct commercial sales (DCS).

Building partner capacity (BPC) is another key term used throughout this monograph. The 2006 Quadrennial Defense Review (QDR) and the 2006 BPC Execution Roadmap emphasize the importance of building the security and defense capabilities of partner countries that will enable them to make valuable contributions to coalition operations and improve their own indigenous capabilities.[6] Building partner capacity is a term of art employed to describe "targeted efforts to improve the collective capabilities and performance of the Department of Defense and its partners."[7] BPC can be thought of as an umbrella objective that draws on the elements of security cooperation. The primary goal of BPC is to implement a multiagency approach to meeting U.S. strategic objectives—one that includes not only U.S. government entities but also key partners and allies abroad. BPC at its best tends to emphasize the "fit" between U.S. regional objectives and the capacity being built or expanded. Programs described as BPC ideally seek to embrace the partner's ability to contribute to U.S. strategic goals.

Several other key terms used here relate directly to assessment issues addressed in this monograph. The terms include *funding source, initiative, program, activity,* and *event*. In the absence of official definitions in a security cooperation context, the study team developed its

---

[5] U.S. Department of Defense, *Security Assistance Management Manual (SAMM),* DoD 5105.38-M, 2009. A full listing of security assistance programs may be found on p. 33 of the SAMM.

[6] U.S. Department of Defense, *The Quadrennial Defense Review Report,* Washington, D.C., February 16, 2006a; and U.S. Department of Defense, *Building Partnership Capacity Roadmap,* Washington, D.C., September 2006b. The QDR and the roadmap represent an evolving concept. They not only include guidance on how DoD should train and equip foreign military forces but also discuss the need to improve the capacity of other security services (i.e., stability police, border guards, and customs) within partner countries. Moreover, the concept also refers to the need to improve DoD's ability to conduct integrated operations with nonmilitary forces (i.e., U.S. interagency, nongovernmental organizations, coalition partners, and the private sector).

[7] U.S. Department of Defense, 2006b, p. 4.

own. The misuse of these terms causes confusion in strategy formulation and policy coordination, which then affects the security cooperation assessment process.

Funding sources are large umbrella resource streams that authorize resources for initiatives or programs. The Freedom Support Act (FSA), which authorizes many security cooperation initiatives and programs in Eurasia, is an example of a funding source. For example, FSA authorizes funding for the State Department's (DOS's) Export Control and Related Border Security Program.

Initiatives are funding sources for a collection of programs that pursue a particular set of goals. Examples of initiatives include the Warsaw Initiative Fund (WIF), which funds programs in central and southern Europe as well as Eurasia, and the Cooperative Threat Reduction program. WIF funds some Air Force security cooperation activities, such as Regional Airspace Initiative studies that have taken place in eastern Europe.

Programs, the focus of this monograph, can be thought of as activities or events coordinated to achieve a set of objectives. Programs have the following defining characteristics, at a minimum:

- mission and set of specific objectives
- activities or events
- managers for policy or resource oversight
- reporting requirements to an oversight agency or office.

Some programs have their own line items in the DoD budget and therefore do not have to solicit funds from other sources to undertake activities. Examples include the Military Personnel Exchange Program (MPEP), managed by the Deputy Under Secretary of the Air Force for International Affairs (SAF/IA), and the UNIFIED ENGAGEMENT Building Partner Capacity seminar series, managed by the Air Staff Concepts, Strategy, and Wargaming Division (AF/A5XS), both of which are funded from the Air Force's operations and maintenance (O&M) budget.

Some programs rely on such sources as initiatives or other programs for funding. Examples include the Regional Airspace

Initiative, mentioned above, funded by OSD's WIF; most programs undertaken by the Air Force component commands, such as chairman's exercises, funded by the Joint Staff; and military-to-military contacts, which are often funded by traditional COCOM activity (TCA) resources.

It is also noteworthy that different offices or individuals may be responsible for policy and planning, resource management, and program execution within organizations and at different organizational levels. Examples are the security assistance programs, such as FMF, FMS, and IMET, all of which are undertaken by DoD but funded and overseen by DOS. The main point to remember from an assessment perspective is that virtually all security cooperation programs have multiple stakeholders.

Activities and *events* are elements of a particular program and are directed, funded, and supervised by program managers. Activities are generic (e.g., Air Force operator-to-operator [ops-to-ops] staff talks), whereas events are specific (e.g., United States–Chile ops-to-ops staff talks). Table 1.1 shows the relationships among funding sources, initiatives, programs, activities, and events using some examples.

Understanding the Air Force's Security Cooperation Mission and Stakeholders

As reflected in national- and department-level strategic guidance, security cooperation continues to grow in importance and emphasis in the planning and operations of all branches of the U.S. armed forces.[8] With greater demand for global reach and a wider net cast for adversaries, conditions, and crises that could threaten U.S. national interests, the 2006 QDR articulated the need to enlist partners to both increase and diversify the capabilities needed to fight "the Long War." As direct threats to the homeland and other national interests continue to arise from dispersed, networked, nonstate actors, it will become increasingly difficult to use U.S. military power alone to "assure, dissuade, deter, and defeat," particularly in unfamiliar geographical and cultural

---

[8] Strategic guidance is provided in the National Security Strategy, National Defense Strategy, National Military Strategy, and GEF.

Table 1.1
Distinguishing the Term

Term	Defining Characteristic	Example
Funding source	Money	Freedom Support Act
Initiative	Money and broad goals	WIF
Program	Specific mission/objectives, manager, activities, reporting requirements	OSD Defense and Military Contacts Program
Activity	Specific interactions funded by programs that include U.S. and partner representatives; designed to address specific objectives	Service-level staff talks
Event	Specific activities occurring annually or at other specified regular intervals	U.S. Army-to-Army staff talks with the United Kingdom

terrain.[9] Although relationships can sometimes be challenging, allies and partners can be a force multiplier. Without reliable predictions of the sources of future security threats, security cooperation efforts help hedge against future security requirements. Hedging can involve establishing new relationships with countries with which the United States has little experience of cooperation.

Air Force Security Cooperation Program Objectives

According to Air Force Policy Directive (AFPD) 16-1, the U.S. Air Force is responsible for conducting international activities to further the warfighting capability of U.S. coalition partners in a way that supports and enhances collective security and regional stability.[10] Allied air force modernization is encouraged to foster commonality, compatibility, and interoperability between U.S. forces and allies within legal, fiscal, and political boundaries. The Air Force is to seek international cooperation

---

[9] The White House, *National Security Strategy of the United States of America,* Washington, D.C., 2002, p. 29.

[10] U.S. Air Force, Office of the Secretary of the Air Force, "Operations Support International Affairs," AFPD 16-1, August 16, 1993. Currently under revision.

and influence through U.S.-based and foreign exchange and training programs.[11]

Air Force security cooperation programs have particular objectives that are designed to be consistent with service, COCOM, and OSD guidance. For example, according to Air Force Instruction (AFI) 16-107, the Air Force MPEP is intended to

- promote mutual understanding and trust
- enhance interoperability through mutual understanding of doctrine, tactics, techniques, and procedures of both air forces
- strengthen air-force-to-air-force ties
- develop long-term professional and personal relationships.[12]

These objectives can be linked to the Air Force end state of establishing, sustaining, and expanding mutually beneficial global partnerships, as well as to the GEF end state of influencing the behavior of key nations.[13] That said, program objectives, including several of those listed above, are almost as vague as the ends they are supposed to support, making credible programmatic assessment impossible without the development of appropriate, accepted, and concrete indicators of performance and effectiveness.

Key Security Cooperation Stakeholders

This brief section provides a short introduction to key security cooperation stakeholders. Chapter Two provides greater details on the specific DoD and Air Force stakeholders.

State Department. Much of the authority for security assistance rests with DOS, which has the final say on Title 22 programs and funding. The ambassador and the country team have a stake in which

---

[11] U.S. Air Force, 1993, paragraph 3.

[12] U.S. Air Force, *Military Personnel Exchange Program (MPEP)*, AFI 16-107, 2006a.

[13] *End states* is but one term of art found in security cooperation documents. Others include *goals*, *objectives*, and—among COCOMs—*effects*. This plethora of terms introduces ambiguity into the body of security cooperation guidance. For example, are *goals* and *objectives* synonyms for *ends* in the prevalent ends-ways-means rubric, or do these terms represent some other thought?

DoD activities are conducted in their country. Country team support is essential for FMS and some DCS programs as well.

DoD. DoD has continued to add emphasis and substance to security cooperation guidance. As the author of the GEF, DoD has a stake in ensuring that COCOMs and the services implement guidance, including the requirement for assessments, and has a major role in the allocation of resources.

Deputy Under Secretary of the Air Force for International Affairs. Within the Air Force, SAF/IA is

> responsible for oversight and advocacy of Air Force international programs and policies [and] will develop, disseminate and implement policy guidance for the direction, integration and supervision of Air Force international programs and activities, [including] political-military affairs, security assistance programs, technology and information transfer, disclosure policy and related activities, international cooperative research and development efforts, attaché and security assistance officer affairs, [among others].[14]

In executing its responsibilities, SAF/IA works with the DOS, OSD, the Air Staff, the component commands, the COCOMs, as well as security assistance officers, attachés, and other Air Force personnel stationed overseas. The existence of so many stakeholders naturally poses challenges to the Air Force in effective coordination and overall efficiency of Air Force security cooperation efforts.[15]

Although SAF/IA has overall policy coordination responsibilities, several aspects of Air Force security cooperation efforts are conducted outside SAF/IA's purview. For example, in addition to the numerous security cooperation–related program elements managed by SAF/IA, the Deputy Chief of Staff, Operations, Plans, and Requirements (A3/5) manages regional security cooperation Title 10 activi-

---

[14] U.S. Air Force, 1993.

[15] Objective 1 of the SAF/IA Strategic Plan (2008) (which is not available to the general public) discusses the need to establish and develop relationships with attachés, security assistance officers, and regional experts.

ties (e.g., UNIFIED ENGAGEMENT, BPC seminars, and ops-to-ops talks that do not directly involve SAF/IA oversight.

Air Force Component Commands. In addition to SAF/IA's security cooperation oversight responsibilities, the Air Force component commands within the COCOMs also have security cooperation responsibilities at the theater level. However, the Air Force component commanders also have difficulty tracking all of the security cooperation activities within their areas of responsibility (AORs), especially those not originating from within the component command. For example, in the European theater, the U.S. Air Forces in Europe (USAFE) commander has limited visibility into all U.S. activities with partner air forces in his theater. Examples of such activities include the National Guard State Partnership Program and the MPEP.[16]

Combatant Commands. From a theater perspective, it is critical to ensure the assignment of an appropriate level of forces to support the security cooperation mission. Forces and force structure are frequently reallocated for operational purposes, often at the expense of the security cooperation mission. It is important to note that four of the six geographic COCOMs—European Command (EUCOM), Africa Command, Southern Command (SOUTHCOM), and Northern Command—are focused primarily on their security cooperation missions. Although the other two geographic COCOMs—Pacific Command (PACOM) and Central Command (CENTCOM)—have demanding operational mission requirements, they also are focused on security cooperation efforts. The COCOMs' respective Air Force component commands follow suit. It is critical that the Air Force component commands receive the appropriate resources (via the lead major command [MAJCOM], Air Combat Command) to ensure that the Air Force effectively supports the COCOMs' security cooperation goals around the globe.

Security Cooperation Guidance

The OSD GEF (2008) states that security cooperation is to be viewed as a campaign-level mission. As a result, several steps have been taken

---

[16] Discussions with senior USAFE officials, Ramstein Air Base, Germany, July 2008.

within DoD in recognition of the elevated importance of the security cooperation mission. In particular, OSD created a new capabilities portfolio called "Building Partnerships,"[17] which elevates the security cooperation mission to a higher level. The portfolio will eventually be able to highlight resource deficiencies for security cooperation in the various DoD program objective memoranda. BPC is also a Joint Staff joint capability area. In addition, OSD-led working groups have been established to develop action plans for resourcing security cooperation in a more institutionalized way.

SAF/IA has been asked to provide the Air Force with input for the Building Partnerships Portfolio, including detailed information on the security cooperation programs that are managed exclusively by the Air Force.

At the service level, the Air Force has taken a number of steps to elevate the importance of security cooperation efforts under its guidance. Specifically, the Air Force now includes security cooperation in the Annual Planning and Program Guidance (APPG), a move that elevates security cooperation to the level of the Air Force's other key planning responsibilities, including readiness, sustainability, force structure, and modernization. In the new Air Force strategy, building partnerships is mentioned as a priority and as an Air Force core function called "Building Partnerships." As a result, the numbered air forces (NAFs) now are told explicitly to include their security cooperation requirements in their input to the Air Force's budget. Also in 2008, SAF/IA updated the Air Force Security Cooperation Strategy (AFSCS), now named the "Global Partnership Strategy."[18]

Moreover, the SAF/IA is working closely with the HQ AF/A3/5 to develop an Air Force version of the Theater Security Cooperation Management Information System (TSCMIS) that will link up with the OSD-led effort to connect all COCOM, service, and DoD agency

---

[17] The Building Partnerships Portfolio is one of nine portfolios within the OSD-led Capabilities Portfolio Management process.

[18] At the time of our research in fiscal year (FY) 2008, the AF Security Cooperation Strategy was the current guidance. The AFGPS was signed into guidance on December 18, 2008, after the research for this study had concluded. As a result, we refer to both documents throughout this monograph.

security cooperation databases in a global TSCMIS. This effort, once completed, will help Air Force stakeholders gain a more complete picture of current security cooperation activities in a given country or theater, or throughout the world.

On a program level, SAF/IA manages a number of Air Force programs, including the MPEP, the Attaché Program, the International Affairs Specialist Program, the Technology Transfer Program, and the Latin American Cooperation (LATAM Coop) Program. However, of these programs, SAF/IA is the program element monitor (PEM) for only the Technology Transfer Program. PEMs oversee the allocation of the program element and also act as advocates for its funding. For the other programs, SAF/IA's role is limited to indirect management, by advocating its priorities to the other PEMs.[19] As part of this effort, SAF/IA develops country plans to help PEMs identify and influence Air Force security cooperation priorities within the DSCA-led process.

Air Force and Security Cooperation Assessments

Security cooperation assessments are needed to help Air Force and other decisionmakers make informed decisions about security cooperation goals, programs, activities, and events. From a program perspective, assessments contribute to decisions about

- how to improve security cooperation programs
- when and whether to continue, cut, expand, or compare security cooperation programs and their subordinate activities, or
- whether to initiate new programs and activities when gaps are identified by the assessment; such gaps might be capability-related or country/regionally related.

The point of conducting assessments is to support decisionmaking with respect to the program at hand. *Thus, stakeholders need assessments only to support the decisions they confront.* Therefore, stakeholders must

---

[19] However, SAF/IA does manage the budget for the LATAM Coop Program for SAF.

fully understand their roles as defined by the relevant legal and regulatory authorities that govern the programs on which they are working. The stakeholders' authorities lead to the program decisions they must make. Once the stakeholders' roles are determined, a seamless assessment is then contingent on a strong understanding of the relationships between the various stakeholders.

This understanding of stakeholder roles will enable stakeholders to conduct assessments that support decisions within their areas of responsibility. For example, lower-level tactical training units within the Air Force that are responsible for training foreign F-16 pilots should not be concerned with assessing the longer-term *outcomes* of that training, such as whether the country provided those trained pilots to a coalition operation at a later time. Rather, the tactical training unit should be looking at the immediate *outputs*, for example, whether the right numbers of pilots were trained, whether proficiency levels increased as a result of the training, and whether the course curriculum was appropriate for the skills sets of the incoming pilots.

For the security cooperation programs in which the Air Force has considerable management authorities, i.e., control of resources and ability to set the objectives, a comprehensive assessment by the Air Force is appropriate. However, for the programs in which the Air Force plays a supporting role to another entity, the Air Force's assessment responsibilities will only be one element of a larger DoD or U.S. government assessment process.

Challenges to Assessing Air Force Security Cooperation Programs

Security cooperation assessments are not easy. Their complexity causes many stakeholders to shudder at the very idea of assessing how well their individual activities are meeting department-level goals and national security objectives. Identifying and substantiating the linkages between programs and objectives rely as much on logic and experience as on quantitative analysis. It is important for assessments to be systematic and as comprehensive as possible, and not based on isolated anecdotes or individual intuition.

Assessment terminology also can be confusing. Several types of assessments—needs, capabilities, performance, and effectiveness—and different units of analysis—country, regional, program, or collection of activities funded by different programs—can be applied. The Air Force must conduct all of these security cooperation assessments to some degree, but it is complicated to determine *who* should be assessing *what* and *how* the results should be collated at the higher levels. To make things even more confusing, OSD guidance is not explicit about how to assess and what exactly to report on, beyond general program outputs.[20]

Individual stakeholders who may be required to conduct assessments often must satisfy multiple masters with differing assessment interests or priorities. Some actors may be interested in assessing the "inputs" or the resourcing aspects of security cooperation, especially the funding and the manpower required to execute a particular program or event. Others might be interested in a top-level country (e.g., Ukraine), or regional (e.g., the Black Sea) assessment, which would entail an examination of the broad range of activities focused on that country or region and might include an effort to assess changes in the Air Force's or the U.S. government's relationship with that country over time. Others might be focused only on the performance of the team that executes the security cooperation activity. And yet others might be primarily concerned with assessing needs or capabilities in individual countries or regions.

To illustrate, the Air Force component commands must answer to two authorities: the highest authority is the COCOM, which looks to the components for country-level assessments. The next is Air Force Headquarters, particularly SAF/IA and the Air Staff, which are primarily interested in program-level assessments, something the component commands rarely consider.[21] In addition to satisfying those assessment requirements, the components are almost universally concerned with securing adequate resourcing (i.e., funding and manpower) for security cooperation activities, given the increased emphasis on this

---

[20] OSD is working to improve its program assessment guidance in the GEF and RAND is assisting in this effort.

[21] We learned this during numerous discussions with Air Force COCOM officials and senior leadership in 2007 and 2008.

mission in recent years. The challenge for the components is to identify ways to collect the necessary assessment data to satisfy *both masters* while also attempting to minimize the manpower needed to conduct the assessments.

Clearly, conducting assessments to satisfy these different expectations requires distinctive assessment designs in each case. Each assessment depends on receiving reliable supporting data, some of which may be quite difficult to collect, especially if authorities have not previously directed the collection and preservation of the information.

At present, Air Force organizations have varying degrees of capabilities to conduct assessments. According to Air Force officers with whom we spoke on this issue, there are several problems: too few organizations/staff sections devoted to assessment; organizational decisions to limit the size of these offices; too few personnel assigned to these organizations; and inadequate training and education and lack of expertise in operations research.

Another challenge worth noting is the emerging requirement for Air Force stakeholders to receive some level of assessment training. It would be helpful if every Air Force stakeholder understood security cooperation assessments and assessment methodologies to some degree, regardless of whether they have a planning, executing, or facilitating role. The emerging demand for assessments may require that Air Force personnel receive further education so that they can be better prepared to perform assessment-related tasks for their security cooperation roles.

Objectives and Key Research Questions

This monograph identifies the kinds of security cooperation assessments that the Air Force should conduct that would be consistent with the intent and spirit of the OSD GEF and the AFGPS. Specifically, the monograph will describe, illustrate, and provide options for implementing an assessment framework for Air Force security cooperation programs.

The monograph considers the following key questions:

- How should the Air Force assess its security cooperation programs and activities?
- Is there more than one assessment approach to consider?
- Should the Air Force assess the programs it manages in a different way from the programs it does not manage?
- How should the Air Force determine which security cooperation stakeholders should conduct the appropriate assessments?
- How should the Air Force ensure that its activities align with OSD and COCOM requirements and assessment processes?
- What Air Force-specific assessment guidance should be provided by Headquarters Air Force to Air Force stakeholders?
- What kinds of assessment questions and indicators are appropriate?

Research Design and Approach

The RAND study team undertook a number of analytic activities to accomplish the study objectives outlined above. The team conducted a literature review of national, DoD, and Air Force strategic guidance on security cooperation assessments. The team also focused on the academic and business assessment literature, especially on qualitative assessment processes. Team members spoke extensively with key policy, resourcing, and assessment personnel and policy planners and implementers in the Air Force, the COCOMs, OSD, the component commands, Combined Joint Task Forces, in-country teams, and other stakeholders in the field.

The study team developed the security cooperation assessment framework and specific recommendations for the Air Force, which will be explained in detail in subsequent chapters.

Organization of the Monograph

Chapter Two provides an overview of the key elements of the Air Force security cooperation assessment framework, which include the strategic guidance, stakeholders, programs, authorities, and resources, associated with Air Force security cooperation programs and activities.

Chapter Three introduces the principles of assessment as found in the academic literature and lays the groundwork necessary to relate those principles to Air Force security cooperation. The chapter introduces a *hierarchy of evaluation*, a concept that is central to the assessment framework, and focuses the assessment on informing policymakers on the decisions they need to make.

Chapter Four illustrates the assessment framework as described in Chapters Two and Three by examining three examples of Air Force security cooperation programs and subsequent activities. The analysis is both illustrative and descriptive and provides insights into the stakeholders and their respective processes for each of the three programs selected as case studies.

Chapter Five describes ways the Air Force can implement the security cooperation assessment framework, as described in Chapters Two and Three and illustrated in Chapter Four. The approach considers the different types of security cooperation programs in which the Air Force is involved, the different kinds of assessment that are possible, the relationships that might be built, and the data that would have to be collected to conduct useful assessments. Chapter Six consolidates and presents the study team's overall conclusions and recommendations.

Appendixes A, B, and C provide further background information. Appendix A provides an illustrative list of Air Force security cooperation programs found in the three categories discussed throughout the monograph: (1) Title 10 programs managed by the Air Force, (2) Title 10 programs not managed by the Air Force, and (3) Title 22 Security Assistance and other DOS-managed programs. Appendix B provides background information for the nine program case studies reviewed for this monograph and illustrated in Chapter Four. For each case, the following information is included: program stakeholder, objectives, processes in terms of how the program operates, resources, and any assessment activities that are currently ongoing. Appendix C provides illustrative examples to suggest how the Air Force might assess the need for a program and its design and theory.

CHAPTER TWO

The Key Elements of Air Force Security Cooperation

To understand the study team's proposed framework for assessing Air Force security cooperation programs, it is important to have a thorough understanding of the key elements of Air Force security cooperation. This chapter thus provides a comprehensive profile of the stakeholders and instruments that enable Air Force security cooperation. The chapter begins with the expectations—that is, key assumptions—that underpin these programs. It then describes each of the key elements, which include the strategic guidance that directs these efforts; the stakeholders involved; the instruments, such as the programs; and the authorities and resources associated with Air Force security cooperation programs and activities.

Guiding Expectations

Air Force security cooperation is animated by the expectation that international activities involving the Air Force and friendly foreign militaries will serve the U.S. national interest. Security cooperation provides a host of programs (described below) that, when executed ably with a friendly partner country, can result in the Air Force being granted access to that state's territory, its airspace, and its installations, thus enabling Air Force operations. Some security cooperation programs seek to improve the partner air force's operational capabilities, with the expectation that eventually the partner air force will be able to offer some support to the U.S. Air Force—perhaps by allowing it to use its bases, or in some advanced cases, by participating in operations with the U.S. Air Force.

Expectations for security cooperation go beyond the partner air force and extend to the partner government itself. By embracing the partner country air force through a wide variety of programs and activities, the U.S. Air Force seeks to eventually influence the outlook of the partner country and, over time, help it to view the world in terms favorable to the United States, adopt policies that are consistent with the interests of the United States, cooperate actively with the United States, and provide the capability and capacity to promote stability and good governance. Successful security cooperation programs contribute to healthy, habitual relationships between the United States and the partner country and contribute to the partner's continued alignment with the United States on matters of mutual importance.

Strategic Guidance

As noted in Chapter One, Air Force security cooperation is part of the Department of Defense's broader security cooperation effort and thus must be responsive to guidance from a number of sources. The point of the guidance is to ensure that Air Force security cooperation programs contribute to the overall U.S. effort, as illustrated in Figure 2.1.

The figure is best understood from the bottom up, where security cooperation tools are mobilized to engage partner countries. These tools generally fall into categories known as security cooperation "ways," as detailed at the bottom of the figure. The Air Force applies these tools to influence the OSD focus areas for security cooperation; they are meant to help achieve a combatant commander's end states or goals, which may be country or regionally oriented or functionally oriented (e.g., emphasizing access to airfields or airspace, enhanced host nation capabilities, and so on). Progress toward a combatant commander's end states or objectives collectively is expected to support the overall U.S. objectives in the international arena.

Figure 2.1
Air Force Security Cooperation Supports Higher Goals

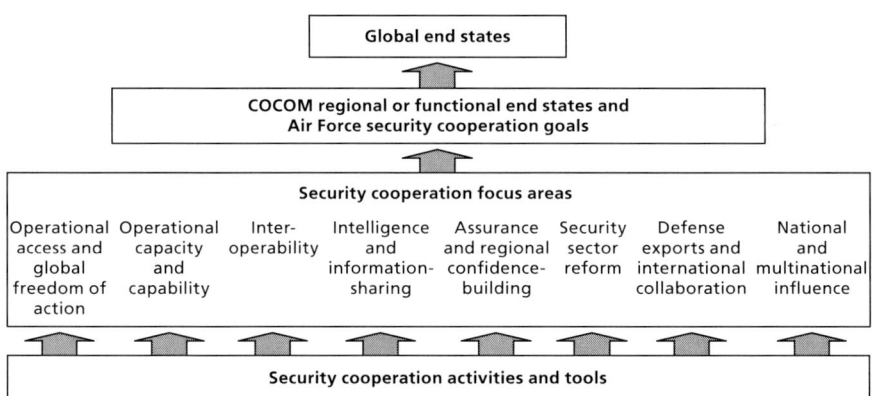

Ways = education, equipment, exercises, experimentation, training, defense and military contacts, personnel exchanges, facilities and infrastructure, information and intelligence cooperation, international agreements, international armaments cooperation, humanitarian assistance, workshops, conferences, and seminars.

SOURCE: Adapted from Tim Hoffman, "Guidance for the Employment of the Force," paper presented at the ODASD Partnership Strategy Worldwide Joint Training and Scheduling Conference, September 17–21, 2007.
RAND *MG868-2.1*

Global End States

In recent years, DoD guidance has emphasized the importance of security cooperation as a key element of a U.S. security strategy. Until 2008, OSD's Security Cooperation Guidance (SCG) spelled out the global end states that guided the multitude of DoD security cooperation programs and activities. This document included four overarching goals or ends:

- assure our allies and partners
- dissuade potential adversaries
- deter aggression and counter coercion
- defeat adversaries.

The SCG focused heavily on building the defense capabilities and capacities of U.S. allies and partners to support partners' internal security needs, regional initiatives, or participation in future coalitions.

This focus on BPC is evident in the "themes" associated with each of the four end states. For example, to assure allies and partners, the SCG called for DoD components to help reform the defense establishments of selected partner countries and build partner capacity to conduct peace and stability operations.

In late 2008, the SCG was superseded by the GEF, which attempts to integrate top-level DoD operational and security cooperation planning efforts.

Combatant Command Regional or Functional End States
At the time of the writing of this monograph, the COCOMs had not yet completed their processes of developing theater campaign plans aligned with OSD's Guidance for the Employment of the Force.[1] Thus, the existing COCOM regional and functional end states are derived from OSD's 2006 SCG as well as the strategic perspectives of individual theater commanders. Although these end states differ somewhat by region and some remain classified, the following are the seven strategic objectives (along with exemplary strategic effects) that EUCOM promulgated in August 2006:

- The United States, its citizens, and interests are secure from attack (e.g., adversaries do not employ strategic weapons to attack the United States or its interests).
- Success is achieved across the range of operations (e.g., EUCOM shapes theater conditions for military success).
- Strategic access and freedom of action are secure (e.g., potential adversaries do not obstruct the strategic reach of EUCOM or U.S. allies and security partners).
- Terrorist entities are defeated and the environment is unfavorable to terrorism (e.g., partner nations increase their capability to combat terrorism).

---

[1] The OSD deadline for the COCOMs to complete the theater campaign plans was November 2008. Campaign support plans, developed by the functional commands, the services, and the defense agencies, were due in early 2009, but that deadline has slipped to later in the year.

- Security conditions are conducive to a favorable international order (e.g., nonstate actors do not impose their will through violence).
- Strong alliances and partnerships effectively contend with common challenges (e.g., NATO extends its sphere of stability beyond Western Europe).
- Transformation leads to evolving challenges (e.g., multinational organizations and the interagency community participate in evolving cooperative security partnerships.[2]

Air Force Security Cooperation Goals

In an effort to keep Air Force security cooperation initiatives in concert with OSD's SCG, in 2006 SAF/IA drafted an AFSCS that included overall goals closely matching the basic SCG pillars described above. These goals include

- building, sustaining, and expanding relationships that are critical enablers for the Air Force
- building future coalition partners by
  - increasing contact
  - building confidence
  - improving capabilities
  - developing compatible concepts of operation.[3]

The AFSCS placed considerable emphasis on the aerospace requirements of emerging partners as well as on increasing the Air Force's ability to support low-end partners faced with domestic security challenges.

To make the AFSCS more service-centric and complementary to the Air Force's operational efforts, strategists in SAF/IA used the six Air Force distinctive capabilities as the building blocks for increasing

---

[2] General William Ward, "The USEUCOM Strategic Effectiveness Process," *Joint Forces Quarterly*, Issue 44, 1st Quarter 2007, p. 55.

[3] U.S. Air Force, 2006b.

partnership capacity and integrating partner capabilities. These capabilities are

- air and space superiority
- precision engagement
- rapid mobility
- global attack
- information superiority
- agile combat support.[4]

The introduction of these capability areas provided an opportunity to bolster the linkage between Air Force security cooperation activities and the operational activities that the Air Force performs in support of the COCOMs. Furthermore, a clear connection to recognized Air Force capabilities helped bring security cooperation strategy and resourcing objectives into closer alignment with the concerns of officials on the Air Staff charged with overseeing the Air Force's planning, programming, budgeting, and execution (PPBE) system.

The 2008 AFGPS, also developed by SAF/IA, replaced the AFSCS and makes BPC the centerpiece of Air Force security cooperation activities. Described as a critical link between national-level strategy and Air Force campaign support plans, this Air Force document establishes the following BPC-related end states:

- Mutually beneficial global partnerships are established, sustained, and expanded.
- Global partners have the capability and capacity to provide for their own national security.
- The capacity to train, advise, and assist foreign air forces, and conduct security cooperation activities using airmen with the appropriate language and cultural skills, is established.

---

[4] U.S. Air Force, 2006b.

- Partnership interoperability, integration, and interdependence are developed and enhanced.[5]

As with previous DoD and Air Force strategic guidance, the AFGPS does not provide specific, measurable objectives that tie security cooperation end states to the programmatic activities being carried out by various executing agencies. Without such measurable objectives, Air Force security cooperation programs cannot be credibly assessed. Fortunately, the Air Force may be on the verge of filling this gap by developing Air Force country pages as part of Knowledgebase.[6] Moreover, it is expected that the new Air Force Campaign Support Plan will include a section on the need to assess program effectiveness. The inclusion of measurable objectives would be a positive addition.

Air Force Security Cooperation Tools—"Ways"

As Figure 2.1 indicated, Air Force security cooperation tools are often characterized as "ways" and typically represent categories of activities that the Air Force undertakes with a partner air force in pursuit of Air Force security cooperation goals or "ends." Thus, there emerges a ways-means-ends relationship in which "ways," such as education or exercises, organize "means" (security cooperation programs) in pursuit of "ends" or goals.

It has been an accepted practice for major security cooperation organizations (e.g., OSD, the services, COCOMs, and DSCA) to develop their own list of security cooperation ways, which they periodically modify. Fortunately, most of these lists share many elements in common. The following are the security cooperation ways included in the 2008 GEF:

- combined/multinational education
- combined/multinational exercises

---

[5] "U.S. Air Force Global Partnership Strategy: Building Partnership Capability and Capacity for the 21st Century," December 18, 2008, p. ii.

[6] Knowledgebase is a centralized, useful repository of security cooperation data and guidance managed by SAF/IA.

- combined/multinational experimentation
- combined/multinational training
- counternarcotics assistance
- counter/nonproliferation
- defense and military contacts
- defense support to public diplomacy
- facilities and infrastructure support projects
- humanitarian assistance
- information-sharing/intelligence cooperation
- International Armaments Cooperation (IAC)
- security assistance
- other programs and activities.

Despite OSD's stamp of approval and a growing consensus on the need for a standardized list, the GEF categorization of security cooperation ways is unlikely to be definitive. For instance, the current GEF list contains missions, such as counternarcotics and counter/ nonproliferation, that cut across such functions as training and exercises. Furthermore, security assistance is generally considered to encompass all DOS-controlled security cooperation programs, including education, training, equipping, and other kinds of activities. Finally, it is not clear why certain security cooperation ways are excluded from the GEF list. For example, workshops and conferences constitute a large share of Air Force and DoD security cooperation activities, which is functionally distinct from defense and military contacts. Also, equipment should be separated from security assistance, since equipment can be provided using either DoD or DOS authorities and resources. Plus, the provision of equipment is just one component of security assistance.

After numerous informal and formal discussions, we have developed a modified list of security cooperation ways that takes into account the aforementioned objections to the GEF categorization scheme and is generally acceptable to the Air Force security cooperation community. The list includes the following 13 categories:

- education
- equipment

- exercises
- experimentation
- training
- defense and military contacts
- personnel exchanges
- facilities and infrastructure
- information/intelligence cooperation
- international agreements
- international arms cooperation
- humanitarian assistance
- workshops, conferences, and seminars.[7]

The next key element of the assessment framework is to synthesize and convert the imperfectly aligned collection of OSD, COCOM, and Air Force guidance into actual programs that can be measured.

Stakeholders

Stakeholders are those organizations or persons with a role in planning, resourcing, or executing the various security cooperation programs. Stakeholders generally face decisions on a range of security cooperation program considerations, including, as discussed in Chapter Three, the need for the program in the first place, the appropriateness of its design and theory, the value of the program's outputs and outcomes, and even the program's cost-effectiveness. Some stakeholders are concerned with program design; others establish program objectives; still others concentrate on implementing the program and controlling its resources.

Arguably, all Air Force senior leaders have a stake in security cooperation program performance, either because they exercise direct authority over the programs, because they are responsible for some

---

[7] It must be acknowledged that the draft 2008 AFGPS takes a very different approach to selecting the ways for "building, sustaining, expanding, and guiding global partnerships." These ways include BPC, counterinsurgency, communication, engagements, foreign internal defense, global community of airmen, professional development, security assistance, security cooperation, and security forces assistance (or train, advise, and assist).

aspect of program performance, or because they must balance demand for Air Force resources between security cooperation and other Air Force core missions, such as generating airpower in support of U.S. security needs. That said, some stakeholders stand out when it comes to managing security cooperation.

State Department

Much of the authority for security assistance rests with DOS, which has the final say on Title 22 programs and funding. Likewise, the ambassador and the country team have a stake in deciding which DoD activities will be conducted in their country. Country team support is essential for FMS and some DCS programs as well. Although DOS and DoD do not always have the same goals and objectives in a country, there is more overlap than not, including in such areas as improving partner capability and enhancing regional stability.

DoD

Over the last decade, DoD has continued to add emphasis and substance to security cooperation guidance. As the author of current security cooperation guidance and the GEF, DoD has a stake in ensuring that COCOMs and the services implement guidance, including the requirement for assessments, and has a major role in the allocation of resources.

Secretary of the Air Force

As a part of the secretary's statutory role exercising civilian control and oversight of the service, the SAF has a stake in the good functioning of the service and all of its activities, including security cooperation. The secretary is responsible for assuring that Air Force security cooperation, as with all Air Force programs, is consistent with OSD guidance, particularly the national military strategy and its supporting strategy documents, and the GEF.

Chief of Staff of the Air Force

The CSAF holds similar, high-level stakes, although the chief's focus is the presentation of air forces. In particular, the chief assures that security cooperation builds relationships, influence, and access to allied and friendly air force capabilities, facilities, and airspace to enhance the USAF's ability to accomplish its missions.

Combatant Commanders

Although not all of the COCOMs feature Air Force generals as their combatant commanders, they nevertheless have stakes in how Air Force security cooperation performs. Given the GEF, the COCOMs have a stake in ensuring that security cooperation activities help move participating countries in their AORs toward their strategic end states and, ultimately, toward the President's and Secretary of Defense's strategic objectives for the region. Their respective air component commands, which in some instances are also numbered air forces, share the combatant commanders' stakes but must also balance the air component command resources committed to security cooperation against other commitments of equal status, including the global war on terrorism, combating weapons of mass destruction (WMD), and other campaign-level obligations.

Deputy Under Secretary of the Air Force for International Affairs

Within the Office of SAF, SAF/IA constitutes an important stakeholder. Its stakes include, for example:

- supervising Air Force security cooperation programs to ensure that security cooperation produces military public goods—capabilities that ultimately all of the COCOMs desire and consume (e.g., space-based systems) but that none were able to identify as requirements within their own planning
- publishing appropriate guidance for the execution of Air Force security cooperation activities in a timely manner
- ensuring that senior Air Force leaders are kept apprised of the Air Force security cooperation activities under way with all U.S. allies and participating partner countries.

For example, SAF/IA is an important stakeholder for Air Force–related armaments cooperation programs, such as the Wideband

Global Satellite (WGS) Communications (SATCOM) Program with Australia, as well as the MPEP Program. As mentioned above, SAF/IA also plays an important role in developing Air Force policies regarding security assistance execution and in ensuring that the service complies with various aspects of U.S. law related to the transfer of military equipment.

Deputy Chief of Staff for Air, Space, and Information Operations, Plans, and Requirements

The Air Staff, particularly the office of the Air, Space, and Information Operations, Plans, and Requirements (AF/A3/5), remains an important stakeholder. Its stakes have to do with the effective coordination and synchronization of its security cooperation activities with the other Air Force participants and the balancing of competing priorities to see that Air Force equities are safeguarded. It has a stake in seeing that the other stakeholders, especially the Air Force MAJCOM and agency stakeholders, receive the accurate, timely information they need to fulfill their own functions within the security cooperation domain. In addition, Headquarters Air Force Regional Plans and Issues Division (HQ AF/A5XX) is an important stakeholder in Air Force staff talks, including CSAF Counterpart Visits, operator-to-operator talks, and airman-to-airman talks.

Air Component Commands

The component commands are also important stakeholders in Air Force security cooperation. They have a stake in ensuring that the COCOMs are resourced appropriately by the Air Force, in this case, for security cooperation purposes. They also have a stake in ensuring that they are carrying out Air Force security cooperation at the theater level in a way that best supports the COCOMs. They should be efficient in using resources and effective in achieving COCOM objectives in the respective partner countries and communicating the results of their activities to the COCOMs and to Headquarters Air Force, where appropriate.

The remaining actors have stakes in the administrative and technical areas: ensuring that security assistance cases get the best technical advice, ensuring that the various letters of agreement and letters of intent are completed properly, seeing that quotas are filled appropriately, and making sure that the various activities in which they play a key role or for which they are responsible are executed according to the relevant guidance. The following list shows additional security cooperation stakeholders and their stake or interest.

- Air Force Research Laboratory
  - Deploy and support common, interoperable equipment; seek cost savings and sharing; pursue best technologies; supply best defense materiel.
  - Explore opportunities to promote future technology cooperation to enhance standardization and interoperability between the United States, its allies, and other friendly nations.
  - Establish and nurture relationships between the technical communities in DoD and Air Force and those of other countries to promote broader defense relationships and for future acquisitions.
  - Remain abreast of developments outside the United States in defense-related technologies.
- Air Force Materiel Command (AFMC)
  - Assign foreign civilian and military engineers and scientists to DoD (government) research, development, test, and evaluation (RDT&E) facilities and U.S. civilian and military engineers and scientists to foreign defense (government and contractor).
- Air National Guard (ANG)
  - Establish sound management of ANG State Partnership Program.
  - Advance closer relations and interoperability between member countries of the North Atlantic Treaty Organization (NATO) and Partnership for Peace countries.
- Air Force Special Operations Command (AFSOC)
  - Pay, or authorize payment for, the expenses of training special operations forces assigned to that command in conjunction with training, and training with, the armed forces and other security forces of a friendly foreign country.

- Air Force Security Assistance Center (AFSAC)
  - Assign line management responsibility to the MAJCOM having cognizance over the article or service being provided and a security assistance program manager.
- Air Force Security Assistance Training Squadron (AFSAT)
  - Serve as the executive agent for all Air Force–sponsored security assistance training; manages foreign military training effectively.
- Inter-American Air Forces Academy (IAAFA)
  - Conduct education and training with inter-American partners in a way that fosters enduring Inter-American engagement.

Stakeholder Roles

DoD security cooperation is complex and, as a result of this complexity, the roles that stakeholders play are not necessarily constant. Their roles change according to the individual security cooperation program. Consider this example: AFSAT is a primary stakeholder in any program that involves delivering training to a partner, and USAFE is a secondary stakeholder when the training is directed at partner air forces within the EUCOM AOR. However, if the training does not involve partners from within the EUCOM AOR, then USAFE is no longer a stakeholder. Conversely, if the program in question does not deliver training, then AFSAT leaves the picture, no longer a stakeholder of any kind, whereas USAFE may become a primary stakeholder if the program affects its equities with partner air forces within the EUCOM AOR.

Nor are all stakeholders members of the Air Force. As described above, the COCOMs can be significant stakeholders. Their equities in security cooperation may cause them to evaluate security cooperation programs differently or to value some programs more than others. They may also resist taskings and requests for information from the Air Force (or any outside entity), which can become a confounding factor when trying to gather data to support security cooperation assessments. Not mentioned above are such U.S. government organizations as DOS's Bureau of Political Military Affairs, OSD Policy's Office of Partnership Strategy, and the DSCA—which oversee certain security cooperation programs in which the Air Force participates as an implementing agency but does not directly manage. Most of these programs are in the area of security assistance. In such cases, Air Force organizations are secondary stakeholders and should expect to respond to the assessment requirements of other agencies that are primarily responsible for security assistance policy and resources.

Also not mentioned above are partner country air forces and security establishments. Although obviously an essential component of the security cooperation process, partners fall into a different category of stakeholder than do U.S. government agencies, since their security cooperation requirements may not fully align with U.S. government strategy. Also, partners cannot be tasked to provide information on the performance or effectiveness of U.S.-managed security cooperation programs. That said, Air Force security cooperation program assessments at any level cannot be considered well-informed without obtaining the perspectives of the partners involved in or affected by the programs under evaluation. This can be accomplished directly by Air Force stakeholders or indirectly through non–Air Force stakeholders, such as geographic COCOM officials or military representatives on U.S. embassy country teams.

Air Force Security Cooperation Programs

Populating the aforementioned categories of security cooperation "ways," programs represent the intersection of authorization for specific security cooperation activities, the assignment of authority over and responsibility for those activities, and allocation of resources from within the budget to support them.[8] As discussed in Chapter One, programs typically have a mission and a set of objectives, a set of subordinate activities or events, managers for policy and resource oversight, and a requirement to render periodic reports to some oversight agency

---

[8] A more detailed discussion of Air Force security cooperation programs can be found in Appendix A.

on the program's performance. Program-level assessment allows the Air Force to take a global view of its security cooperation mission by

- facilitating decisions about continuing, expanding, or cutting programs and resources devoted to security cooperation
- providing insights into the authorities, roles, and responsibilities of multiple security cooperation stakeholders
- recognizing the need to balance requirements among countries and regions as well as security cooperation and operations.[9]

Before attempting to categorize the variety of Air Force security cooperation programs, it is necessary to define what a program is in terms of assessment. This is important because the term *program* is used indiscriminately in military strategy and policy documents and in conversations among government officials and national security analysts.

Unfortunately, a singular definition of the term *program* is impractical because of the different mechanisms by which security cooperation is authorized, funded, managed and executed. In some cases, such as the Air Force's MPEP, a program is an actual line item in the Air Force's program objective memorandum and in the DoD portion of the Presidential Budget. In other cases, such as Air Force staff talks and UNIFIED ENGAGEMENT BPC Regional Seminars, a program is an interconnected series of activities or events funded through the Air Force's O&M account and other sources. In still other cases, such as the support and training provided by the Air Force to the Canadians following their purchase in 2006 of Boeing C-17 cargo aircraft, a program is a major FMS case funded by a partner country.

To further complicate matters, government documents often describe all FMS itself as a single program. In our view, FMS, which

---

[9]   By acknowledging the utility of programmatic assessment, we do not intend to belittle the importance of country or regional assessments of U.S. security cooperation activities. These kinds of assessment have their purpose, especially in helping to determine security cooperation outcomes in particular places. Ideally, they should be accomplished in coordination with programmatic assessments using the same basic data elements. Generally, however, country assessments should be performed by Air Force elements in the field, with direct and ongoing interaction with foreign partners, under the guidance of the COCOMs, as opposed to Air Force security cooperation officials based in the United States.

funds thousands of DoD-managed security assistance projects, is best described as a funding source, not a program, for assessment purposes. We consider major FMS cases, such as the Poland F-16 case, to be a program for assessment purposes.

The same can be said for other forms of security assistance, such as IMET. We consider IMET training provided to a specific country to be a program for assessment purposes. Initiatives such as the WIF, a compendium of programs designed to provide assistance to countries seeking cooperative military and peacekeeping relations with NATO and overseen by OSD, generally are too large and varied to be assessed as a whole. However, the individual programs funded by WIF, such as the Regional Airspace Initiative Program, would be considered a program for assessment purposes. Additionally, regional or countrywide security initiatives, such as the Georgia Train and Equip Program and Plan Colombia, do not meet our definition of program. Rather, they are collections of programs, activities, and resources cobbled together by the executive branch or Congress.

That said, neither we nor the Air Force can have the final word on this topic. A standard program definition, acceptable to all major security cooperation stakeholders, is needed before programmatic assessment can be conducted in a comprehensive and analytically defensible fashion.

Authorities

Recognizing the authorities under which security cooperation programs operate is essential to creating an appropriately tailored assessment framework for the Air Force. As Chapter Three will explain, "one size fits all" assessments are usually unworkable for such complex organizational efforts as security cooperation, which involves many kinds of programs, various stakeholders, and multiple layers of bureaucracy. Thus, the first step in determining assessment responsibilities is to organize programs in accordance with legal, policy, and regulatory authorities. However, annual legislation may terminate a program's authority or funding or may authorize new programs. Many of DoD's current authorizations and funding have come from legislative initiatives over the past few years and must be renewed annually to continue. In the case of security cooperation, programs generally fall under two major titles of the U.S. Code (U.S.C.): Title 10 and Title 22.[10] Consistent with those titles, the Air Force also has published its own directives and regulations to govern the way that most of its security cooperation programs are managed and executed.

U.S.C. Title 10

Title 10 is the basic authority for most Air Force roles in raising, training, and maintaining military forces and also serves as the primary authority for many Air Force security cooperation programs. A program that typifies this type of security cooperation is the LATAM Coop Program, which is chartered to "advance the influence and prestige of the United States and the U.S. Air Force within Latin American countries." U.S.C. Title 10, §1050, authorizes service secretaries to "pay the travel, subsistence, and special compensation of officers and students of Latin American countries and other expenses the secretaries consider necessary for Latin American cooperation." According to 1987 amendments to the Latin American Cooperation Act, "funds for the conduct of exchanges, seminars, conferences, briefings, orientation visits, and other similar activities are made available to each of the military departments." Military departments, in turn, distribute the funds throughout each of the departments for funding the security cooperation program.

As is the case with other service-managed Title 10 programs, the authorities governing LATAM Coop give the Air Force and the other military departments, particularly the Army, the primary responsibility for controlling resources, developing policies and objectives, and implementing the program. Like LATAM Coop, several Air Force–managed Title 10 programs are intended to promote defense and military contacts. Others focus on personnel exchanges (e.g., the MPEP);

---

[10] Title 32 might also be included, as this provision governs the National Guard Bureau. However, from a security cooperation context, only one National Guard program, the State Partnership Program, falls under Title 32.

conferences, seminars, and workshops (e.g., the UNIFIED ENGAGE-MENT seminars); defense and military contacts (e.g., Air Force ops-to-ops talks); and IAC (e.g., U.S.-Canada Defense Development Sharing Program); among other security cooperation "ways."

The Air Force does not fully manage all of the Title 10 security cooperation programs in which it participates. For example, OSD Policy is primarily responsible for the WIF and several other Title 10 programs for which the Air Force has an execution role. Another example is the Chairman of the Joint Chiefs of Staff (CJCS) exercise, FLEXIBLE RESPONSE, in which the Joint Staff and EUCOM are the principal DoD stakeholders. In neither case does the Air Force determine overall policy objectives.

However, elements of the Air Force can and do play an important role in resourcing, designing, and implementing WIF, CJCS, and other security cooperation initiatives and programs that are not managed by the Air Force. These include, for example, the five DoD Regional Centers for Security Studies, Foreign Disaster Assistance, the Global Train and Equip Program, and the Commanders Emergency Response Program. As will be explained in Chapter Five, the distinction between programs managed by the Air Force and programs not managed by the Air Force figures prominently in determining which organizations should be responsible for assessing which aspects of a program.

U.S.C. Title 22

Title 22 provides the basic authority for security assistance. A distinctive component of security cooperation, security assistance is under the policy and resourcing control of DOS, but it is administered by DoD. In contrast to Title 10 security cooperation activities whose principal focus is improving the ability of DoD to perform its missions by working with allies and partners, the purpose of Title 22 security assistance is to support U.S. foreign policy goals by focusing on the needs of foreign partners and international organizations. Title 22 security assistance programs and funding sources include FMS, FMF, IMET, DCS, presidential drawdown, excess defense articles, and equipment leases.

FMF is a pool of U.S. security assistance resources that partner nations use to purchase military training, equipment, and other services through FMS or DCS cases. Thus, two sources of funding can finance military equipment sales: the partner countries' national accounts or the U.S. taxpayer through FMF. Title 22 requires presidential approval of FMF for procurement of defense articles, defense services, and design and construction services by partner countries and international organizations.[11] FMF funding is appropriated by Congress annually through the Foreign Operations Appropriations Act based on DOS's budget request. The FMF budget request is currently a joint effort between DOS and DoD. DoD's inputs are a collaborative effort between OSD policy, the COCOMs (represented by the Joint Staff), and DSCA, which manages the FMF account. As the value of security cooperation programs have grown, the COCOMs, including their respective Air Force components, have become a strong voice in this process.

The Security Assistance Organizations' (SAOs') military personnel in U.S. embassies overseas coordinate FMF details with recipient countries. FMF funding is appropriated by Congress annually through the Foreign Operations Appropriations Act based on a budget request prepared jointly by DOS and DSCA. The military services, including the Air Force, exert influence over the development and design of FMF cases through the Letter of Offer and Acceptance (LOA) process with the partner country. As implementing agencies, the services also bear direct responsibility for delivering the materials or services set forth in the LOA.[12]

The other major source of security assistance funding is IMET, which provides grant financial assistance for training in the United States and, in some cases, in overseas facilities to selected foreign military and related civilian personnel. Although IMET receives its funding and policy guidance from DOS, it is managed by DSCA in coordination with the SAOs, the COCOM, and the services. The Air Force and other military departments are responsible for the implementation of approved training, including assessing proposed international

---

[11] U.S.C. Title 22, §2763.

[12] Deputy Under Secretary of the Air Force for International Affairs, *SAF/IA Security Assistance Handbook,* November 17, 2000, p. 21.

student qualifications, matching students with available training positions, and monitoring student progress.[13]

Air Force Governing Directives

The Air Force publishes its own directives to delegate authority from SAF and CSAF to their subordinates to manage security cooperation generally and to promulgate instructions for the specific conduct of Air Force–controlled security cooperation programs. For example, the Air Force has issued AFPD 16-1 appointing SAF/IA as the principal office to manage, direct, and establish policy for international affairs.[14]

The Air Force publishes similar directives and guidance for each security cooperation program it manages or implements. For example, AFI 16-107 describes the basic responsibilities of Air Force organizations involved in the MPEP.[15] In the case of this Title 10, Air Force–managed program, SAF/IA generally coordinates the selection and assignment of exchange officers, both U.S. Air Force and foreign, based on recommendations provided by the air component commands. Regional program management officers (PMOs) are responsible for the day-to-day administrative support of U.S. Air Force officers assigned in their region, and continental United States (CONUS) PMOs provide similar support to foreign officers assigned to U.S. Air Force units. The 474th Operations Group Personnel Exchange Program (474 OG/PEP) at Davis-Monthan Air Force Base, Arizona, for example, hosts the CONUS PMO responsible for the daily oversight of foreign exchange officers assigned to the SOUTHCOM AOR.

It should be noted that not all Air Force–managed security cooperation programs have published instructions. For instance, Air Force UNIFIED ENGAGEMENT seminars are not governed by any published directives but instead are planned in coordination with the COCOMs and component commands. HQ AF/A5XX exercises overall responsibility for seminar content.

---

[13] U.S. Air Force, "International Affairs and Security Assistance Management," Air Force Manual (AFM) 16-101, 2003a, p. 12.

[14] U.S. Air Force, 1993. Currently under revision.

[15] U.S. Air Force, 2006a.

By contrast, some Title 10 security cooperation programs that are executed but not managed by the Air Force have Air Force governing directives. For example, AFI 10-204, *Readiness Exercises and After-Action Reporting Program*, explains how the Air Force participates in exercises, including such combined exercises as the previously mentioned FLEXIBLE RESPONSE. USAFE, in its supplement to this document, assigns primary responsibility for planning and oversight of this participation to the Exercise Division (HQ USAFE/A3X). Within HQ USAFE/A3X, the Joint Exercise Branch (HQ USAFE/A3XJ) is the office responsible for overseeing the USAFE portion of FLEXIBLE RESPONSE. Much of the actual planning and development of the exercise, however, is conducted by Third Air Force (3 AF), with the 3 AF Directorate for Operational Analysis (3 AF/A9) leading this effort.[16]

The *SAF/IA Security Assistance Handbook*[17] outlines the major roles and responsibilities of Air Force organizations involved in the implementation of Title 22 security assistance programs. In particular, within SAF/IA, the Policy Directorate develops Air Force policy and coordinates policy compliance for FMS, and the Regional Affairs Directorate develops, coordinates, and ensures the implementation of Air Force system sales to foreign customers. The Assistant SAF for Acquisition works with SAF/IA to review cases of customer requests for system sales. The Deputy Chief of Staff for Plans and Requirements (HQ USAF/A5) assesses the effect of foreign customer requests on Air Force operations, including participation in Air Force exercises. AFSAC directs the letters of offer and acceptance process for system sales. AFSAC also supports system program directors, security assistance program managers, and SAF/IA in their review of system sales cases. Product centers, under AFMC, are responsible for systems management. For example, the 516th Aeronautical Systems Group (AESG), at Wright-Patterson Air Force Base, Ohio, manages acquisition programs for aeronautical systems and their components, such as

---

[16] Discussions with USAFE officials, June 2008.

[17] Deputy Under Secretary of the Air Force, 2000.

the C-17 transport aircraft, for the Air Force and such partner countries as Canada.

Security Cooperation Resources

Funding for security cooperation resides in a number of subactivity groups and program elements within the defense budget. Unfortunately, most of these groups or elements do not directly correspond to the Air Force security cooperation programs described in this chapter. For example, the Miscellaneous Support to Other Nations Sub-Activity Group funds OSD-directed missions in support of other nations to promote regional stability and shape the international security environment in ways that favor U.S. national security. In particular, this Sub-Activity Group provides administrative and logistics support and civilian pay for security cooperation programs, such as the previously mentioned LATAM Coop Program, that foster important military interactions between the United States and its multinational partners. Funding for the Miscellaneous Support Sub-Activity Group totaled $427 million in 2008, an undetermined amount of which was directed to the Air Force.[18]

Another way to slice the defense budget is by strategic account. Within the 2008 research and development (R&D) account, there are 16 budget lines related to international cooperation totaling $1.06 billion, of which the Air Force directly manages three lines totaling $8.94 million, or less than 1 percent. The program elements associated with these lines include International Space Cooperative R&D and NATO R&D.[19] Within the O&M account, there are several budget lines related to international cooperation totaling $7.17 billion, of which the Air Force controls directly $59.56 million, again, less than 1 percent of the total. Examples include Air Force ops-to-ops and UNIFIED ENGAGEMENT seminars. Thus, insofar as can be determined from

---

[18] The source for all budget figures cited in the following paragraphs is the DoD FY 2008 budget.

[19] Program Elements 0603790F and 0603791F, respectively.

an analysis of the DoD budget, the Air Force is responsible for $68.5 million in Title 10 security cooperation funding.

Determining the total amount of funding devoted to security cooperation is complicated by DoD's practice of embedding funds for some security cooperation activities in budget lines without a clear connection to security cooperation. Moreover, the SAF enjoys great flexibility to reprogram funds to meet operational requirements. Depending on the specific account and the program category (O&M, military personnel, RDT&E, etc.), the secretary may reprogram funds of up to $10 million and sometimes $15 million. In some instances, the secretary is also obliged to provide a follow-on report within 30 days to explain the progress or outcome associated with the reprogramming action. In other instances, the secretary may require prior approval from Congress, while in still other circumstances—those not otherwise constrained by law—the DoD comptroller is the ultimate authority and no approval from Congress is required.[20]

These budgeting complications can make it difficult to conduct certain kinds of assessments. Specifically, without the easy ability to align dollars with programs, it can be very difficult to assess costs and benefits, inputs and outputs, and trade-offs that might reveal opportunity costs associated with security cooperation decisions, depending on the level within the chain of command at which the assessments are attempted. Financial management officials reveal they have very little awareness of security cooperation funding beyond the activities and programs for which they have direct responsibility.

To a certain extent, Title 22 security assistance funding is easier to determine than Title 10 funding. Although more recent information is not available, in FY 2004 the Air Force was allocated the following amounts for FMS execution by organization:

- SAF/IA—$6.7 million
- AFMC—$69.4 million

---

[20] Specific congressional authority is required to transfer funds between appropriations and between subdivisions within them. General Transfer Authority (GTA) normally appears in the annual DoD Appropriations Act and the National Defense Authorization Act.

- AFSAT—$3.3 million
- others—$2.9 million
- SAF/IA and AFSAT—$98,000 and $860,000 additional, respectively, for FMF execution in FY 2004.[21]

These funds are from the annual FMS budget approved by Congress and managed by DSCA. Although these funds are not part of the Air Force's table of allowances, assessments should assist Air Force stakeholders in their budget requests to DSCA and improve the process for partner nations using the Air Force FMS system.

The money budgeted for developing, executing, and sustaining specific FMS/FMF cases is not visible to the public, although presumably it can be found in DSCA's security cooperation database. Despite the fact that DOS is required to provide Congress with a detailed annual breakdown of security assistance training dollars by foreign partner, this information is not associated with implementing agencies, such as the Air Force. Finally, a full accounting of the facilities, personnel, and O&M costs to the Air Force MAJCOMs for training foreign partner air force units, such as Polish F-16 pilots and logisticians, is only beginning to be attempted by Air Force organizations such as USAFE.[22]

Conclusions

This chapter is intended to provide a baseline understanding of the key elements of Air Force security cooperation before the proposed framework that follows in subsequent chapters is described. Through this description, an appreciation of the complexities of security cooperation emerged: the different meanings associated with the term *program*, the complicated funding streams and programmatics that make it difficult to align funding with programs, and the dynamic nature of

---

[21] Deputy Under Secretary of the Air Force for International Affairs, "Air Force Security Assistance Resource Board Briefing," Washington, D.C., December 3, 2003.

[22] Discussions with USAFE officials, Ramstein Air Force Base, Germany, July 2008.

stakeholders and their stakes, which change depending on the authorities governing different security cooperation programs. Each of these emergent complexities ultimately manifests itself as a constraint on the Air Force's ability to assess its security cooperation. Nevertheless, all of the key ingredients are there—guidance and authorities. There is an appreciation of the value of assessments by Air Force stakeholders, and we have found many positive local attempts to conduct assessments. The need to identify all of the programs and resources devoted to security cooperation activities is understood. There is a sense within the Air Force security cooperation community that assessments are needed and desired. The next chapter outlines the basic principles of assessment as they pertain to Air Force security cooperation.

CHAPTER THREE

Principles of Assessment for Security Cooperation

Supported by a firm understanding of the key elements of Air Force security cooperation and the different security cooperation roles and relationships that Air Force organizations might undertake, the discussion now turns toward assessment. What is assessment and what purposes does it serve? More specifically, what aspects of security cooperation can be assessed and to what ends? This chapter introduces the principles of assessment as found in the academic literature on evaluation research and lays the groundwork necessary to relate those principles to Air Force security cooperation. The chapter presents a *hierarchy of evaluation*—a concept that is central to the assessment framework and serves as a useful tool for appropriately matching types of assessment with specific stakeholder needs.

What Is Assessment?

Assessment is research or analysis to inform decisionmaking. When most people think of evaluation or assessment, they tend to think of outcomes assessment: Does the subject of the assessment "work"? Is it worthwhile? Although this is certainly within the purview of assessment, assessments cover a much broader range and can be quite varied.

Most assessments are conducted using research methods common in the social sciences. However, evaluation and assessment can be distinguished from other forms of research by their purpose. Assessment is fundamentally action-oriented. Assessments are conducted to determine the value, worth, or effect of a policy, program, proposal, practice, design, or service with a view toward making decisions about changing that program or program element in the future. In short, *assessments must be explicitly connected to informing decisionmaking.*

Within the action-oriented/decision support role, assessments can differ widely. Assessments can support decisions to adjust, expand, contract, or terminate a program. They can support decisions regarding which services a program should deliver and to whom. And they can support decisions about how to manage and execute a program.

Assessment is not new to the Air Force. The Air Force does a great deal of assessment in domains other than security cooperation (e.g., check rides and operational readiness certifications). Furthermore, several Air Force organizations (the Inspector General [IG], the Air Force Audit Agency [AFAA], etc.) conduct certain kinds of assessments routinely. Note that the examples above are assessments, because they involve research in support of decisions. For example, in the case of check rides and audits, the decisions supported include whether a pilot will be certified and allowed to fly missions and whether legal proceedings or other remediation will be pursued with regard to mismanagement of funds.

Why Assess?

Although some decisions can be made based on ad hoc or intuitive assessments, many demand assessments that are based on more extensive or rigorous research methods. Where important decisions are to be made and ambiguities exist about the factual bases for those decisions, assessment is the antidote.

Across most aspects of government and military activity, there are regular calls for assessments; security cooperation is no exception. The OSD GEF, as part of elevating the prominence of security cooperation (as discussed in Chapters One and Two) explicitly calls for delivering annual assessments to OSD. In addition to this high-level call for security cooperation assessment, security cooperation practitioners are well aware of the frequency with which stakeholders request (or require) further assessment-related reporting. Quality assessment of security cooperation programs will contribute to improved decisionmaking at all levels, including oversight, planning, management, resourcing, and execution.

Principles of Assessment and Evaluation Research

Evaluation research describes a well-established area of social science scholarship focused on assessment. Although evaluation research methods have been applied to a host of contexts and problems, the paradigmatic case for evaluation research is a public policy program, such as a smoking cessation program or an adult literacy program. One can easily imagine a range of evaluative questions one might want to ask to guide decisions about such programs:

- How extensive is community need for a cessation program?
- How effective is the program at getting people to stop smoking?
- Who from the target population is participating in the program?
- Is the program delivering the counseling and other services it is supposed to?
- What fraction of those who start the program complete it?
- What is the cost per individual completing the program?
- Should public funding be used to support smoking cessation?

Although these questions differ substantially in scope and focus, they share the common thread of assessment: *a connection to specific decisions.*

Good evaluation research always informs decisionmaking. The policy areas, levels, and specific decisions informed by evaluation research can differ widely: Assessment could help decisionmakers decide whether to continue or cancel a program, improve the management of resources for a program that is not meeting process targets, or make decisions about the audience at which a program is targeted. Assessment helps answer questions about the status and effectiveness of a program (i.e., how are we doing?), about the reasons for observed levels of effectiveness (i.e., what is going wrong?), and about improvement (i.e., what do we need to change to make it work?).

Fortunately, Air Force security cooperation activities are sufficiently allied to public policy programs by nature that the language and approaches of evaluation research remain broadly applicable. The detailed evaluative questions will differ slightly, as will the specific policy decisions that assessments are meant to inform. Assessment methods will remain largely the same. Similarly, the overall goal of assessment should remain the same: *Air Force security cooperation assessments should explicitly connect to informing decisionmaking.*

Connecting Evaluation Research and Security Cooperation

One core challenge in developing security cooperation assessment strategies for the Air Force is identifying the decisions that need assessment support. Effective assessment and evaluation can be critical tools for informed decisionmaking and policymaking; conversely, mismatched assessments can be worse than useless. That is, mismatched assessments do not add value to management or decisionmaking but *do* cost time and other resources to generate. With that concern in mind, what kinds of assessments of Air Force security cooperation efforts are appropriate and useful? Evaluation research suggests a supporting question: What kinds of decisions need to be made about the programs and activities that constitute Air Force security cooperation?

Stakeholders Versus Assessment Stakeholders

Being a "stakeholder" in an assessment and evaluation context takes on a definition narrower than that in common usage. In broad application, as discussed in Chapter Two, a stakeholder in a program is a person or organization that affects or might be affected by the actions of that program. *Assessment stakeholders* are persons or organizations that make decisions for or about a program. This narrower definition helps keep assessment focused on decisions. Ancillary common-use stakeholders who are curious about a program or who are downstream and are affected by a program but do not get to make or contribute to decisions are not assessment stakeholders. They may provide data that contribute to assessments, but they should not be defining assessment needs.

Challenges to Security Cooperation Assessment

To understand the decisions that need to be made for and in oversight of Air Force security cooperation activities, one must identify the activities themselves, enumerate the stakeholders for those activities, and carefully match stakeholders' decisional needs with appropriate levels and types of evaluation. But a handful of challenges facing Air Force security cooperation assessment activities must be overcome, worked around, or otherwise dealt with to achieve full success in this regard. These are discussed in detail below and again in later chapters to help illustrate and implement the assessment framework. These challenges have been identified through discussions with key Air Force and other DoD personnel and through the research and analysis performed by the study team members in this and prior study efforts focused on developing security cooperation assessment frameworks. The assessment framework developed in this monograph is intended to help overcome these challenges.

Determining Causality. Arguably the biggest challenge confronting security cooperation assessment lies in trying to identify causality: linking the activities of specific security cooperation programs to specific advances toward COCOM or U.S. end states (outcomes). The abundance of U.S. security cooperation initiatives—from DOS, other DoD programs, the U.S. Agency for International Development, and the Departments of Justice, Homeland Security, Energy, Treasury, and Commerce—confounds our ability to assign causality, as do various exogenous factors, such as international politics, global public diplomacy, etc. As Chapter One noted, the best we can hope for at the outcomes level in many instances is to find some relationship between success in security cooperation programs and progress within security cooperation focus areas.

Paucity of Well-Articulated Intermediate Goals. We have asserted that assessment must be tied to decisionmaking. However, a critical assessment challenge is to know what kinds of information these decisions should be based on. For example, it is fairly intuitive to decide whether to continue an effort based on whether it is working. However, it is analytically very difficult to tell whether something is working when causal connections are conflated with other activities (or exogenous factors) or end states and goals are very high level, opaque, difficult to measure, or require only that a program or activity contribute indirectly.

Well-articulated intermediate goals that programs can directly contribute to are important facilitators for effective program assessment. If a program can be shown to be meeting (or not meeting) clearly stated intermediate goals, decisions can be made about meeting those goals differently, meeting them more efficiently, or making the changes necessary to begin to meet them satisfactorily (if they are not being adequately met). However, where such goals are lacking, decisions are difficult to support with assessment.

In many instances in security cooperation, concrete intermediate goals are underspecified. High-level guidance documents such as the GEF provide important overarching themes and desired ends but do not provide sufficiently detailed or specific goals for individual programs. Program managers or executors may (or may not) develop sets of targets or short-term goals, and these may or may not have a clear connection to the highest-level guidance. Clear expressions of how exactly individual Air Force efforts are supposed to contribute to larger OSD and Air Force goals and end states would facilitate many forms of assessment at many different levels.

Assessment Capabilities of Air Force Stakeholders. It takes effort to both collect and analyze raw data to produce completed assessments. Resource constraints can adversely affect the quality of data collection; if a program executor has to choose between completing an assessment questionnaire well and getting started on the next major program activity, assessment quality may suffer.

Different Air Force organizations have different levels of preparation and capability for assessment. Some security cooperation programs either have regular access to the Strategic Plans and Programs Directorate in the Air Staff (HQ AF/A8) and the Air Force Studies and Analyses, Assessments, and Lessons Learned Directorate (HQ AF/ A9) personnel who help with assessment, or have sufficient manning (and foresight) to build up a staff dedicated to assessment. Other programs are very tightly staffed, having just a few personnel with multiple responsibilities and working long hours before assessment even enters the picture. The Air Force is mixed in this regard. As discussed in Chapter Five, some Air Force organizations are wholly devoted to conducting certain kinds of assessment that potentially can be used for security cooperation assessments.

Good assessment planning and assessment matching can ease the resource burden. Relevant personnel will be better able to plan for and complete assessment data collection if they know beforehand the period or event for which they will need to collect data. A single set of coherent assessment data requests requires less time to complete than a host of different and partially duplicative or partially useless calls for assessment data.

Multiplicity of and Differing Priorities of Stakeholders. Air Force security cooperation programs have many stakeholders. Decisions for and about these programs are made by many organizations at many levels. The constellation of stakeholders differs from program to program depending on the relevant authorities and relationships, as discussed in Chapter Two.

Although the inclusion of many stakeholders is not inherently challenging, it can complicate assessments in a number of ways. First, personnel at the program execution level can have multiple masters each with different goals. This can complicate assessment when stakeholders request different but similar assessments using different processes. Second, a single organization can have different "stakes" as a stakeholder in different programs. For instance, one could have a "supporting" role relative to one program and a "supported" role for another. Thus, an assessment might not be viewed consistently within a single organization.

Third, stakeholders can have different priorities for security cooperation programs. As the old saying goes, "where you stand depends on where you sit." Some stakeholders may harbor contradictory stakes and, hence, priorities. Numbered Air Forces that also serve as the air component command for a COCOM may be a case in point. As a numbered air force, the organization may assign a high priority to its operational missions, such as its ability to provide combat air forces and fulfill its role in the broader tapestry of the Air Force's Title 10 commitments. At the same time, as the air component command within a COCOM, it may also have competing priorities to marshal its resources in support of security cooperation programs that build partner capacity with other countries' air forces. Such competing and perhaps conflicting priorities could easily color the organization's view of security cooperation and the value of security cooperation program assessment; it might view the entire assessment effort as a distraction, for example, if concerns about its Title 10 commitments dominate its thinking. Alternatively, the organization may welcome security cooperation assessments if it views its principal mission as building capacity in partner air forces.[1]

Some Air Force organizations, particularly those created to administer security cooperation programs and activities (such as AFSAT and AFSAC), will have other priorities, perhaps to make security cooperation more efficient or to perpetuate certain programs that, in their professional judgment, yield great dividends for the Air Force. In such instances, priorities would certainly clash if officials at the highest levels were questioning the need for the program or its congruence with Air Force strategic goals while further down the chain of command, stakeholders running the program were striving to maximize its throughput or advocating its expansion if warranted by their judgments of its value.

Fourth, some stakeholders may want to conduct assessments that exceed the scope of decisions they either make or support. Many stakeholders consulted for this study asserted actual stakes in a particular security cooperation program that extend beyond their formal authorities. Many argued that they exercise both formal influence and decisionmaking responsibilities on the basis of their mandate in the Title 10 and Title 22 authorities, but they also exercise informal authority, which most often takes the form of advocacy. That is, stakeholders believe that

---

[1]   Discussions held with USAFE officials in July 2008 suggest that this may be an example of the latter case. Here, the Air Force component focuses on BPC and tends to value its squadrons as the key instruments for this security cooperation activity rather than valuing them for other tasks (e.g., their potential roles in contingency plans).

their jobs involve acting as advocates for decisions and policy options in their interactions with the higher echelons of the chain of command. Therefore, they may want to have at their disposal assessments that are not linked directly to specific decisions and decisionmaking points that lie specifically within their authority. As a result, it often can be confusing to prescribe specific assessments to stakeholders who resist assessment constraints placed by the limits of their formal decisionmaking authorities.

In addition to different policy preferences, these priorities can lead to different and conflicting emphases on different types of assessment questions. Officials in OSD and the COCOMs may not care about the merits of specific security cooperation programs, caring only that they contribute to the overall effort to advance the U.S. position in a given theater. At SAF/IA's level, however, other priorities may dominate, including meeting the service's overall responsibilities to raise, train, equip, and maintain forces; generate airpower in the national interest; or perhaps exploit opportunities with allies to create new military public goods.

Security Cooperation Data Tracking Systems Not Organized for Security Cooperation Assessment. As discussed in Chapter Two, cost-effectiveness and opportunity cost evaluations are difficult to make because funding is scattered across and buried within a number of program elements and budget lines. Some data are maintained in Knowledgebase and in the COCOMs' respective TSCMIS, but not all security cooperation stakeholders provide inputs, nor do they all have access to these systems. As a result, it is not clear that a complete, accurate, current repository of all security cooperation activities and their details (resources involved, place, duration, frequency, etc.) exists.

Sound assessment requires specific information. If Air Force organizations are to become competent at assessment, they must collect and maintain the necessary information to support the assessments they attempt. Currently, instructions mandate the assessments but do not establish requirements to collect the data to support them. In the absence of an official data collection requirement and a plan for harvesting the data, assessments will remain difficult to perform.

Confusing Terminology. The changing lexicon of security cooperation also complicates assessment. New guidance documents invariably alter the language of security cooperation. Some consistency is essential if Air Force organizations are to be able to manage assessments over time as the guidance changes. For example, how might one know if goals and end states are the same or different? Are "goals" and "ends" equivalent? What is the equivalent of "focus areas" in earlier guidance? Misunderstandings along these lines could distort and corrupt assessments by treating terms as if they mean the same thing when in fact they do not.

"Passing the Buck" on Assessments. There is also the practice, widespread within DoD, of delegating the task of assessment to subordinate organizations. Although this practice may be effective at the upper echelons of OSD, within the Air Force it causes trouble for multiple reasons. The first problem is that many of the officers and staffers charged to perform the assessments have operational backgrounds; they are not trained to design and perform assessments. Without an assessment template and a dataset at hand, often they are left to their own devices to conceive and execute the assessment. Even in organizations with appropriately trained staff, the necessary data are rarely fully available and potential sources are not obvious. Moreover, even if officials tasked with the assessment find the organization with the necessary data, they usually cannot compel the organization holding the data to share them. Unless the Air Force makes the effort to specify the types of assessments it expects from particular commands or agencies and takes steps to collect and organize the supporting information, individual offices will have little choice but to continue the common practice of polling subject matter experts for their opinions of how various programs are performing.

Expectations and Preconceived Notions of Assessment. A final challenge faced by security cooperation assessment stems from the expectations and preconceived notions of many stakeholders. There are many different views about what assessment is or should be. Virtually all Air Force officers and senior civilians have some experience with assessment but usually just a limited slice of what is possible under the broad tent offered by evaluation research. A narrow preconception that assessment is only ever one type of analysis or data collection can be limiting. Further, expectations that assessment adds limited value or that it is acceptable to require assessments to satisfy curiosity (rather than to inform essential decisions) can lead to unnecessary evaluations or create resistance to assessment proposals. In fact, assessment is many different things from many different perspectives. Virtually all of these perspectives—provided they pertain to decisionmaking—can be captured in the hierarchy of evaluation, as discussed below.

The Hierarchy of Evaluation

Given the explicit focus on assessment for decisionmaking that comes from evaluation research and the need to connect stakeholders and their decisionmaking needs with specific types of assessment, the Air Force needs a unifying framework to facilitate that matching process. To fill this need, "the hierarchy of evaluation" as developed by evaluation researchers Peter Rossi, Mark Lipsey, and Howard Freeman, is presented in Figure 3.1.[2] The hierarchy divides all potential evaluations and assessments into five nested levels. In this nesting, each higher level is predicated on success at a lower level. For example, positive assessments of cost-effectiveness (the highest level) are only possible if supported by positive assessments at all other levels. Further details appear below in the subsection "Hierarchy, Nesting, and Feedback."

Level 1: Assessment of Need for the Program
Level 1, at the bottom of the hierarchy and foundational in many respects, is the assessment of the need for the program or activity. This is where evaluation connects most explicitly with target ends or goals. Evaluation at this level focuses on the problem to be solved or goal to be met, the population to be served, and the kinds of services that

---

[2]   Peter H. Rossi, Mark W. Lipsey, and Howard E. Freeman, *Evaluation: A Systematic Approach*, Thousand Oaks, Calif.: Sage Publications, 7th ed., 2004.

Figure 3.1
The Hierarchy of Evaluation

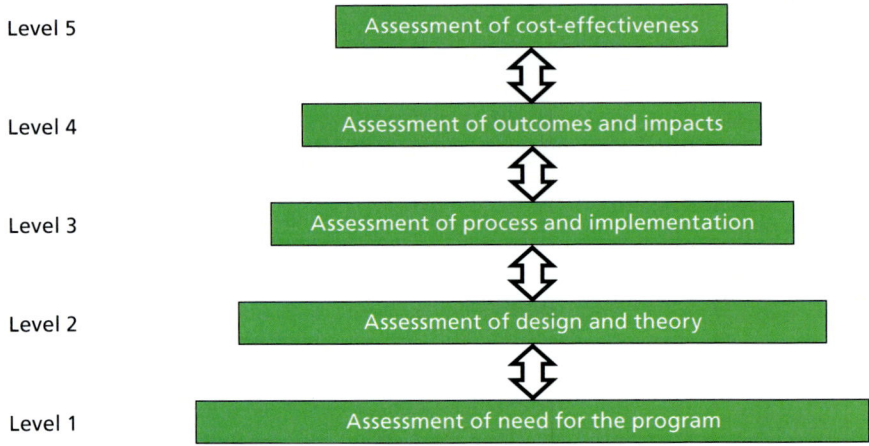

SOURCE: Adapted from Christopher Paul, Harry J. Thie, Elaine Reardon, Deanna Weber Prine, and Laurence Smallman, *Implementing and Evaluating an Innovative Approach to Simulation Training Acquisitions*, Santa Monica, Calif.: RAND Corporation, MG-442-OSD, 2006, Figure 7.1.
RAND *MG868-3.1*

might contribute to a solution.[3] Research questions could include the following:

- What are the nature and magnitudes of the problems to be addressed?
- What audience, population, or targets does the need apply to?
- What kinds of services or activities are needed to address those problems?
- What existing programs or activities contribute to meeting this goal or mitigating this problem?
- What are the goals and objectives to be met through policy or program?

Evaluation of public policy often skips the needs-assessment level, as stakeholders assume the need to be wholly obvious. This is true

---

[3]   Rossi, Lipsey, and Freeman, 2004, p. 76.

broadly in public policy but also in DoD and the Air Force. Where such a need is genuinely obvious or the policy assumptions are good, this is not problematic. Where need is not obvious or goals are not well-articulated, troubles starting at Level 1 in the evaluation hierarchy can complicate assessment at each higher level. As evaluation researchers Richard Berk and Peter Rossi note:

> In the broadest sense, evaluations are concerned with whether or not programs or policies are achieving their goals and purposes. Discerning the goals of policies and programs is an essential part of an evaluation and almost always its starting point. However, goals and purposes are often stated vaguely, typically in an attempt to garner as much political support as possible. Programs and policies that do not have clear and consistent goals cannot be evaluated for their effectiveness. In response, a subspecialty of evaluation research, evaluability assessment, has developed to uncover the goals and purposes of policies and programs in order to judge whether or not they can be evaluated.[4]

Level 2: Assessment of Design and Theory

The assessment of concept, design, and theory is the second level in the hierarchy. Once a needs assessment establishes that there is a problem or policy goal to pursue as well as the intended objectives of such policy, different solutions can be considered. *This is where theory connects ways to ends.*

Assessment at this level focuses on the design of a policy or program. Analyses of alternatives are generally evaluations at this level. Research questions might include the following:

- What types of program are appropriate to meet the need?
- What specific services should be provided, in what quantity, and for how long?

---

[4]   Richard A. Berk and Peter H. Rossi, *Thinking About Program Evaluation,* Newbury Park, Calif.: Sage Publications, 1990, p. 15.

- How can these services best be delivered?
- What outputs need to be produced?
- How should the program or policy be organized and managed?
- What resources will be required for the program or policy?
- Is the theory specifying certain services as solutions to the target problem sound?

Most of the evaluation questions at this level are answered either based purely on theory or based on previous experience with similar programs or activities. This is a critical and foundational level in the hierarchy. If program design is based on poor theory, then perfect execution (of the ways) may still not bring about desired results (the ends). Similarly, if theory does not actually connect the ways with the ends, the program may accomplish objectives other than those it was intended to. Unfortunately, this level of evaluation also is often skipped or completed minimally and based on unfounded assumptions. See the discussion in the next section.

Once a program is under way, design and theory can be assessed firsthand. For an ongoing program, assessment questions at this level could include the following:

- Are the services being provided adequate in duration and quantity?
- Is the frequency with which services are provided adequate?
- Are resources sufficient for the desired execution?

Note that assessments at this level are not about execution (i.e., "are the services being provided as designed?"). Such questions are asked at Level 3. Design and theory assessments (Level 2) seek to confirm that what was *planned* is adequate to achieve the desired objectives.

Level 3: Assessment of Process and Implementation

Level 3 in the hierarchy of evaluation focuses on program operations and the execution of the elements prescribed by the theory and design at Level 2. A program can be perfectly executed but still not achieve its goals if the design was inadequate. Conversely, poor execution can foil the most brilliant design. For example, a well-designed series of military-to-military interactions could fail to achieve desired results if executing personnel did not show up or were late or surly.

Assessment at this level needs to be periodic and ongoing. Just because a program's process goals are being met at one point in time does not necessarily mean they always will be in the future. In addition to measuring process, Level 3 evaluations include "outputs," the countable deliverables of a program. Possible research questions at Level 3 include the following:

- Were necessary resources made available?
- Are the intended services being delivered as designed?
- Are process and administrative objectives being met?
- Is the program being managed well?
- Are service recipients satisfied with their service?
- Were regulations followed?
- Are program resources being used or consumed as intended?

Level 4: Assessment of Outcomes or Effects

Level 4 is near the top of the evaluation hierarchy and concerns outcomes and effects. At this level, outputs are translated into outcomes, a level of performance, or achievement. Put another way, *outputs* are the products of program activities, *outcomes* are the changes resulting from the projects. This is the first level of assessment at which solutions to the problem that originally motivated the program can be seen. Research question at Level 4 could include the following:

- Do the services provided have beneficial effects on the recipients?
- Do the services provided have the intended effects on the recipients?
- Are program objectives and goals being achieved?
- Is the problem at which the program or activity is targeted improving?

Level 5: Assessment of Cost-Effectiveness

The assessment of cost-effectiveness sits at the top of the evaluation hierarchy, at Level 5. Only when desired outcomes are at least partially observed can efforts be made to assess their cost-effectiveness. Simply stated, before you can measure "bang for buck," you have to be able to measure "bang."

Evaluations at this level are often most attractive in bottom-line terms but depend heavily on lower levels of evaluation. It can be complicated to measure cost-effectiveness in situations with unclear resource flows or where exogenous factors significantly affect outcomes. As the highest level of evaluation, this assessment depends on the lower levels, as described in the next section, and can provide feedback inputs for policy decisions primarily based on the lower levels. For example, if target levels of cost efficiency are not being met, cost data (Level 5) in conjunction with process data (Level 3) can be used to streamline the process or otherwise selectively reduce costs. Possible Level 5 research questions include the following:

- How efficient is resource expenditure as measured against outcome realized?
- Is cost reasonable relative to the magnitude of benefits?
- Could alternative approaches yield comparable benefit at lower cost?

Hierarchy, Nesting, and Feedback

This framework is a hierarchy because the levels nest within each other; solutions to problems observed at higher levels of assessment often lie at levels below. If the desired outcomes (Level 4) are achieved at the desired levels of cost-effectiveness (Level 5), then lower levels of evaluation are irrelevant. But what about when they are not?

When desired high-level outcomes are *not* achieved, information from the lower levels of assessment needs to be available for examination. For example, is a program not realizing target outcomes because the process is not being executed as designed (Level 3) or because the program was not designed well (Level 2)? Evaluators have problems when an assessment scheme does not include evaluations at a sufficiently low level to inform effective policy decisions and diagnose problems when the program does not perform as intended. It is acceptable to assume away the lowest levels of evaluation only if the assumptions prove correct. However, when assumptions are questionable, the best risk avoidance strategy is to do assessments at Levels 1 and 2 rather than risk launching a program that is doomed to fail at Levels 4 and 5 because the foundational levels (needs and design) simply will not support overall targets. According to Rossi, Lipsey, and Freeman, programs that fail generally do so because of problems at Level 2 (theory failure) or Level 3 (implementation failure).[5] Good program implementation works only if the underlying program design works.

Feedback from higher to lower levels should also be an important part of the overall assessment process (hence the arrow superimposed on the assessment hierarchy in Figure 3.1). For example, Level 5 cost-effectiveness assessments could be used as inputs to Level 1 need for program assessments, especially in cases where new or proposed programs are being evaluated and data on the program at hand are either scarce or nonexistent.

Generic Security Cooperation Assessment Questions and Data Requirements

As discussed above, each level of the evaluation hierarchy implies a set of generic security cooperation assessment questions, the answers to which will differ considerably depending on the program's nature, the authorities of the stakeholders, and so forth.

Recalling that programs are the unit for analysis, we will need a mechanism that can produce program-level answers to our generic security cooperation questions. In particular, we will want to aggregate individual assessments from individual program events and activities over time—perhaps several years—to produce program-level, time-series insights into the program's performance. Time-series data are expected to reveal trends that will allow the Air Force to determine whether the trajectory of individual security cooperation programs and the trajectory of the relationship with the partner countries are

---

[5] Rossi, Lipsey, and Freeman, 2004, p. 78.

consistent with each other (e.g., generally positive, stable, or generally negative).

Assessments like these can prove complicated, so the supported organizations conducting the assessment have an obligation to develop a careful assessment design and to keep to it, whereas the supporting organizations have an obligation to archive the essential data to fuel the assessment, paying attention to data counting rules: individual attendees versus whole classes, hours of events versus days of events, comparable activities, etc., so that assessments across several years will be able to employ consistent metrics.

Table 3.1 lists the generic security cooperation assessment questions and the types of supporting data that should be maintained to answer them. These generic questions suggest the general classes of questions that a supported (assessing) organization would have to ask at each level of the hierarchy of evaluation. The generic questions could be modified to satisfy the specific information needs of the assessing organization and the specific program. The assessing organization must ask questions whose answers will support decisions related to the program in question.

Getting the Measures Right

Evaluation research methodology encourages the connection of assessment questions to policymaking so that management and other program or policy decisions can be based on evaluation measures. For assessment to contribute effectively, evaluators need not only to ask the right questions but to receive *believable* and *actionable* answers to those questions. Connecting research questions to policy decisions is half the equation and connecting the actual measures and metrics to the research questions is the other.

Evaluators must ask the right questions in the right way and be able to get valid, measurable answers. Berk and Rossi discuss the importance of measurement validity in evaluation research.[6] *Validity* concerns the extent to which a given measure allows the best approximation of the truth for a given inference or conclusion. Validity con-

---

[6]   Berk and Rossi, 1990, pp. 16–17.

Table 3.1
Generic Security Cooperation Assessment Questions and Supporting Data

Questions for Each Level	Supporting Data
Level 1: Need for the Program	
Is demand for the program growing, steady, or shrinking?	Records of demand over time: requests to participate, letters of agreement, letters of intent, etc.
Among all Air Force programs, where does this one rank?	Knowledge of overall Air Force programs and the priority attached to each
If the Air Force faces budget cuts, is this program a bill-payer or a priority for protection?	Knowledge of overall Air Force programs and the priority attached to each
Do other programs produce the same benefits with the same partners?	Knowledge of overall Air Force programs, their participants and benefits
If so, what are the two programs' relative cost-effectiveness?	Cost-benefit/cost-effectiveness data for all USAF programs
Level 2: Design and Theory	
Does logic lead us to expect the outputs claimed for the program, given the inputs to the program?	Security cooperation guidance, program documentation describing goals, and expected contributions of program outputs
Do assumptions linking program performance to security cooperation focus areas appear logical?	Program documentation describing goals and expected contributions of program outputs
Do the claimed associations between security cooperation focus areas and regional/functional end states seem logically consistent?	Program documentation describing goals and expected contributions of program outputs, knowledge of relevant end states
Has the program produced desired outputs or outcomes in the past?	Past performance data for program
Level 3: Process and Implementation	
Is the program resourced sufficiently to perform its functions and activities relative to demand for them?	Demand data, resource data (personnel, materiel, and funding)
Does the program meet deadlines, fill quotas, and otherwise satisfy performance and administrative standards?	Records of administrative and operational performance, attendees, participants, numbers of graduates

Table 3.1—continued

Questions for Each Level	Supporting Data
Does the program observe restrictions and prohibitions with respect to technology transfers and spending constraints?	Export/transfer authority documentation, financial records
Is program execution conducted so as to foster positive impressions of it among its participants?	Exit surveys of participants collected over time to support time-series analysis

Level 4: Outcomes and Effects of the Program

Do participants leave with more skill/ capacity than they arrived with?	Entry and exit testing collected over time to support time-series analysis
Is partner capability in the program's areas growing, stable, or declining?	Time-series data on partner capabilities
Is the program's contribution to security cooperation focus areas growing, stable, or declining?	Measures of performance for focus areas: Access and global freedom of action = number of airfields operational capacity = partner trend data in numbers of certified aircrews, operational aircraft, available airfields, flight hours per year Interoperability = progress over time at reaching numbered levels of interoperability as assessed during field training exercise intelligence and information sharing = trends in frequency and quality of information Assurance and regional confidence building = trends in CSBMs, security regimes, security cooperation activities (frequency, size, number of participants) Security sector reform = trends in adoption of U.S. practices, trends in corruption based on Office of Defense Cooperation, defense attaché reports Exports and international collaboration = trends in numbers of orders placed or filled, size and duration of deployments with U.S. forces National and multinational influence = trends in number of participating countries, number of program activities, and number of participants from each country

Table 3.1—continued

Questions for Each Level	Supporting Data
Level 5: Cost-Effectiveness	
What is the cost per unit of output?	Cost data, data on units of output
How do cost-effectiveness data compare with data from other security cooperation programs?	Cost-effectiveness data on other security cooperation programs
What is return on investment (ROI) for the program?	ROI data
How does ROI compare with that of other Air Force programs?	Cost data for all Air Force programs
Do any other Air Force programs produce the same outputs for less cost?	Detailed cost-process information
What can be done to reduce cost per unit of output?	Detailed cost-process data

cerns the strength of the relationship between what you want to know and what you actually measure. For example, imagine that you want to know whether you should increase or decrease the length (number of sessions) of a smoking cessation program. You measure total sessions attended by program participants and calculate the correlation between total attendance and success at stopping smoking. This approach has "face validity" (it sounds like a logical, appropriate measurement) but that validity could be threatened under several circumstances.

First, total attendance might not reveal *patterns* of attendance that might be useful in decisionmaking. Imagine the different implications of two different attendance patterns at a hypothetical smoking cessation program, both of which involve attending half of the program's scheduled sessions: One participant attends all of the first half of the scheduled sessions and then stops smoking and stops attending; another participant attends every other session (still half of scheduled sessions) and also stops smoking. For these individuals, half the scheduled number of sessions appears to be adequate to achieve the target outcome, but the second individual's attendance pattern might not relate well to a program that scheduled half as many sessions sequentially.

Second, attendance might not have been properly recorded. Session coordinators may have taken attendance at the very beginning or the very end of a session, excluding participants who arrived late or left early.

Third (and similarly), just recording attendance does not capture length of involvement (those leaving early or arriving late) or quality of individual sessions (perhaps sessions 1, 3, 8, and 9 are the most important sessions). A measure that captured this information might suggest that the total number of sessions can be reduced but that the compressed program should include particular sessions.

Fourth, attendance alone might provide limited information to support a decision to extend program length under certain circumstances. If cessation is low even among those with high attendance, this might suggest that a longer program would do better. However, the low success rate might be primarily due to another factor, perhaps even something outside the control of the program. Further thought and additional measurement would be necessary to support such a decision.

Another issue concerns the degree of precision necessary to connect measurement to policy. Some policy decisions require very precise measurement support if assessment is to be effective. For example, efforts to increase efficiency may need very detailed process measurements to identify areas to streamline. Conversely, some policy decisions do not require much precision—"rough and ready" assessment may suffice where only approximate answers are needed.[7] For example, decisionmaking about an inexpensive program might need only vague evidence of a positive effect and not require precise measurement of the magnitude of that positive effect.

There is a substantial body of literature on performance measurement and metrics in a business context, much of which is applicable here.[8]

---

[7]   Berk and Rossi, 1990, p. 10.

[8]   See, for example, Harry P. Hatry, *Performance Measurement: Getting Results,* 2nd ed., Washington D.C.: Urban Institute Press, 2007; Laura H. Baldwin, John A. Ausink, and Nancy Nicosia, *Air Force Service Procurement: Approaches for Measurement and Management,* Santa Monica, Calif.: RAND Corporation, MG-299-AF, 2005; Lisa Diernisse, "Performance Metrics for Non-Mathematicians," *Contract Management Magazine,* Vol. 43, No. 6,

Conclusions

This chapter offered a definition of and a motivation for assessment: Assessment is research and analysis in support of decisionmaking. Drawing on the literature on evaluation research, the chapter identified challenges that Air Force security cooperation efforts face. The hierarchy of evaluation serves as the foundation for our proposed assessment framework because it can be a powerful tool for appropriately matching types of assessment with specific stakeholder needs. The chapter concluded with generic security cooperation assessment questions tied to the hierarchy, which is the cornerstone of the assessment framework that is illustrated in the next chapter.

June 2003, pp. 44–53; and Laura H. Baldwin, Frank Camm, and Nancy Y. Moore, *Strategic Sourcing: Measuring and Managing Performance,* Santa Monica, Calif.: RAND Corporation, DB-287-AF, 2000.

CHAPTER FOUR

Illustrating the Assessment Framework

Building directly on the key elements of Air Force security cooperation introduced in Chapter Two and the hierarchy of evaluation discussion in Chapter Three, this chapter illustrates the assessment framework by examining three case study examples of Air Force security cooperation activities. The analysis is both illustrative and descriptive, as it provides insights into the stakeholders and their respective processes for each program selected. The first section describes the assessment activities that stakeholders should conduct for each of the five levels of analysis. The next section briefly describes the methods used and the case study selection. The following section describes current stakeholder activities for each case study and illustrates how they can be mapped to the assessment framework by linking each stakeholder to the appropriate levels of assessment analysis and the associated generic assessment indicator questions. Finally, the chapter concludes with some specific observations related to the descriptive analysis.

Approach

In close coordination with SAF/IA, the study team initially selected nine security cooperation programs in which the Air Force has a role. Programs were selected to provide examples of each of the three categories described in Chapter Two:

- Title 10 security cooperation programs managed by the Air Force
- Title 10 security cooperation programs not managed by the Air Force
- Title 22 security assistance programs.

In addition, the examples were to incorporate as many of the security cooperation "ways" as possible.[1]

The study team examined these programs to identify the differences between Air Force roles across the three categories and ways.[2] There was no attempt to assess any of these programs. Instead, the team simply identified the stakeholders and their roles as a way to understand how the assessment framework might be applied. As Table 4.1 shows, the cases cover many of the Air Force security cooperation ways.

In developing the sections that follow, however, the discussion is limited to three representative cases:

- ops-to-ops staff talks
- Air Force participation in a CJCS exercise
- FMS support and training case.[3]

Collectively, the programs cover each of the three categories and four of the security cooperation ways.

---

[1] As described in Chapter Two, these include education; equipment; exercises; experimentation; training; defense and military contacts; personnel exchanges; facilities and infrastructure; information/intelligence cooperation; international agreements; IAC; humanitarian assistance; and workshops, conferences, and seminars.

[2] Many programs are worthy of consideration to illustrate the assessment framework outlined in this monograph. The cases we chose cover the three categories, include a variety of stakeholders, and were nominated by different Air Force organizations. Clearly, other cases could have been used. The primary source of information regarding the cases is a series of focused discussions conducted from May through July 2008 with officials from SAF/IA, HQ Air Education and Training Command (AETC)/IA, AFSAT, Air Force Institute of Technology (AFIT), the 373rd Training Squadron (373 TRS), AFSAC, the 516th AESG, HQ AF/A5XX, HQ AF/A5XS, and HQ USAFE/A3XJ (Joint Exercise Branch).

[3] All nine cases are discussed in detail in Appendix B. Questions to guide discussions with stakeholders are also included there.

Table 4.1
Case Studies, by Security Cooperation Way and Program Category

Way	Category 1: Title 10 Security Cooperation Programs Managed by the Air Force	Category 2: Title 10 Security Cooperation Programs Not Managed by the Air Force	Category 3: Title 22 Security Assistance Programs
Training			Canadian C-17 FMS
Education			IMET (AFIT)
Exercises		CJCS Exercise FLEXIBLE RESPONSE	
Exchanges	MPEP		
Conferences and workshops	UNIFIED ENGAGEMENT seminars		
Defense and military contacts	Ops-to-ops talks		
Equipment			Chile F-16 FMS Canadian C-17 FMS Canadian C-17 DCS
Armaments cooperation		WGS SATCOM	

Program Descriptions

This section briefly describes the three featured security cooperation programs selected by the study team. These three programs were
selected because they represent a variety of security cooperation ways
and, more important, they illustrate the different roles that Air Force
stakeholders might have with regard to a program. For example,
the first program, Air Force ops-to-ops staff talks, is an Air Force–
managed program, meaning that the Air Force controls the resources
and decides both the outcome and the output objectives.

The second program is a CJCS exercise led by EUCOM. In this
program, the Air Force is largely reimbursed for its participation, meaning that for the most part it controls resources that belong to another,

non–Air Force stakeholder. Additionally, although it does set output objectives for the exercise, the Air Force does not directly set the outcome objectives. Despite this, USAFE does play a significant role as a EUCOM component command, helping to set the outcome objectives.

Finally, the third program is a Title 22 FMS case designed to support the direct commercial sale of C-17 transport aircraft to Canada. In this program, as with the previous case, the Air Force controls resources that are provided to it by another stakeholder. The FMS case directly funds the acquisition of parts and supplies and also reimburses the Air Force for manpower expenses. Although the Air Force sets output objectives for the program, it does not become directly involved in setting outcome objectives. But, the Air Force can influence these objectives, just not in the collaborative way that occurs in the COCOM-component command relationship as seen with a CJCS exercise.

Air Force Operator-to-Operator Staff Talks

HQ AF/A5XX is an important stakeholder for Air Force staff talks, which include the CSAF counterpart visits, ops-to-ops talks, and airman-to-airman talks. HQ AF/A5XX oversees the ops-to-ops talks by preparing agendas and invitations, arranging the logistics, facilitating the discussions, and following up on action items that result from the talks. These relationships, currently in place with 11 countries, allow talks to take place on a rotating basis with each country participating in talks approximately every 18 to 24 months.[4] The U.S. Air Force delegations are led by an Air Force general officer and typically include one or two subject matter experts, a COCOM representative, a SAF/IA representative, and one officer from HQ AF/A5XX. Partner country delegations are similarly composed. The talks typically consist of a review of the status of any action items taken during previous talks, a discussion of new agenda items, and agreement on any new action items. Other elements can include tours of relevant facilities, social events, and cultural tours.[5]

---

[4] The 11 countries are Australia, Chile, France, Germany, Israel, Italy, Japan, the Netherlands, Singapore, South Korea, and the United Kingdom.

[5] Discussions with HQ AF/A5XX official, July 2008.

Chairman of the Joint Chiefs of Staff Exercise FLEXIBLE RESPONSE

FLEXIBLE RESPONSE is a CJCS exercise conducted annually by EUCOM. The exercise focuses on U.S. and partner responses to WMD attacks against EUCOM assets. Accordingly, one of the primary objectives of FLEXIBLE RESPONSE is to exercise various agreements between the host nations and the U.S. military forces that outline their response to such incidents. For the most part, the responses are simply talked through in detail by U.S. and foreign military leaders, and the interaction between the affected sites is limited to communications between base command posts. This type of exercise is commonly referred to as a command post exercise (CPX). In 2008, the exercise consisted of several separate but related scenarios, including four distributed across USAFE bases in Germany and Italy.[6]

Canadian C-17 Foreign Military Sales Equipment Transfer and Training Case

In early July 2006, the Canadian government announced that it was buying four C-17 Globemaster III transport aircraft from Boeing. The cost of this sale was approximately $3.4 billion, of which about $1.6 billion was for a 20-year maintenance agreement with Boeing.

In addition to purchasing the aircraft through a direct commercial sale, Canada also purchased support and training through an FMS case. The Air Force stakeholders for this FMS effort include SAF/IA, HQ AETC, HQ Air Mobility Command (AMC), AFSAC, the 516 AESG, AFSAT, the 97th Air Mobility Wing (97 AMW), and Detachment 5 of the 373 TRS.

For the support portion of the case, the 516 AESG played a key role, because it serves as the Air Force's C-17 system program office (SPO) and is responsible for all aspects of C-17 system acquisition and sustainment.[7] The group provides C-17 acquisition and sustainment support not only for the U.S. Air Force but also for such partner countries as the United Kingdom, Australia, and Canada. In the Canadian C-17 FMS case, the 516 AESG established the Canada integrated prod-

---

[6] Discussion with HQ USAFE officials, July 2008.

[7] Telephone discussion with 516 AESG officials, July 2008.

uct team (IPT) to handle activities related to the program. The Canada IPT comprises Air Force civilian and military personnel, including a warranted contracting office, a financial management analyst, a budgeting officer, and acquisition and logistics professionals. In addition, four Canadian military personnel are assigned to the office to facilitate interaction with the Royal Canadian Air Force. One of the 516 AESG's key tools is its Globemaster III Sustainment Partnership (GSP) contract with Boeing. The GSP is a contractor logistics support contract, meaning that it is designed to ensure that the Air Force has access to spare parts, necessary repairs, and engineering support for the aircraft. In fact, under the GSP, Boeing even manages the supply chain for C-17 parts, providing warehousing, shipping, and parts management.

A second major piece of the FMS case was training for Canadian aircrew members and maintenance technicians. The flying training was conducted by the 97 AMW at Altus Air Force Base, Oklahoma, and consisted of ground school, simulator training, and actual time flying the C-17 aircraft. The ground school and simulator portion was conducted by contractors, but this is normal for all C-17 flying training and was not unique to the Canadian case.[8] The flying portion was conducted by U.S. Air Force flying instructors, using standard training procedures common to all U.S. Air Force flying training.[9]

The technical training for the maintenance technicians, however, is more specialized and was designed as a unique program for the Canadians. The training was conducted by AETC's Detachment 5 of the 373 TRS at Charleston Air Force Base, South Carolina, an AMC C-17 base. Detachment 5 reports to its parent unit, the 373 TRS, at Sheppard Air Force Base, Texas. Management of the training, therefore, is done by the 373 TRS and, accordingly, the squadron training manager is AFSAT's main point of contact for this case. Although Detachment 5 is tasked with training the Canadian technicians, its personnel also train U.S. Air Force technicians.[10]

---

[8]   Discussion with AFSAT officials, Randolph Air Force Base, Texas, May 2008.

[9]   Discussion with AFSAT officials, Randolph Air Force Base, Texas, May 2008.

[10]   Discussion with 373 TRS official, July 2008.

Linking the Programs to the Levels of the Assessment Hierarchy

For each program considered, the study team initially identified the Air Force stakeholders by reviewing AFPDs and instructions and holding discussions with SAF/IA staff members. AFM 16-101, for example, highlights the responsibilities of several Air Force stakeholders, both for security assistance activities and for other security cooperation efforts, such as exercises, air shows, and competitions.[11] This initial list grew as the team met with representatives from the various stakeholder organizations, which in turn resulted in an even more comprehensive understanding of the key stakeholders involved with the programs. Even so, this list of stakeholders is only representative of the broad range of Air Force organizations involved in some fashion with Air Force security cooperation programs. *The main point is that many stakeholders play many different roles in the development and execution of Air Force security cooperation activities. Decisionmakers must understand these roles to assign assessment responsibilities.*

The discussion below focuses on the key stakeholders and their roles in each of the five levels of analysis. The next five sections illustrate the actions undertaken by the key stakeholders in three key Air Force security cooperation programs and demonstrate how those actions can be associated with a level of analysis.

Level 1: Assessment of Need for the Program

This section describes how key stakeholders conduct needs assessments for Air Force security cooperation programs. Implementing an assessment framework first requires an understanding of the stakeholders and the kinds of decisions they need to support with assessment and the types of activities that characterize those stakeholder roles. As they conduct these activities, stakeholders should gather data that will help them answer assessment questions. Chapter Three presented a set of

---

[11] Competitions, when they include foreign air forces, are a form of defense and military contacts. AFM 16-101 states that competitions provide an "opportunity for both USAF and international participants to enhance operational capabilities, interoperability, and coalition operations" (U.S. Air Force, 2003a).

generic assessment questions for each of the analysis levels, which are repeated below in Table 4.2 to illustrate the types of assessment interests that each stakeholder should have in relation to the actions they are taking. Throughout this and the following sections, we will illustrate how the key stakeholders could use these illustrative questions at each level of analysis. At the end of the chapter, a summary table lists each stakeholder, the levels at which they are involved, and the assessment questions they should be concerned with.

Table 4.2
Stakeholders and Needs Assessment Questions

Program	Stakeholder	Assessment Question	Illustrative Answer
Ops-to-ops staff talks	AF/CV Headquarters Air Force Regional Issues Division	Is demand for the program growing, steady, or shrinking?	Judging by partners' growing inability to fill quotas, dwindling country nominations, and declining interest from COCOMs, demand for program is shrinking
CJCS Exercise FLEXIBLE RESPONSE	USAFE Third Air Force Vice Commander Third Air Force Directorate of Operational Analysis	Among all Air Force programs, where does this one rank?	Program is consistent with OSD's number 2 priority, AF/CV's top priority, and EUCOM/CENTCOM top priorities
Canadian C-17 FMS support case	Air Force International Affairs AFSAC 516 AESG	If the Air force faces budget cuts, is this program a bill-payer or a priority for protection? Do other programs produce the same benefits with the same partners? If so, what are the two programs' relative cost-effectiveness?	Program consumes only $6.2 million but provides otherwise unobtainable access to state-of-the-art foreign technology; AF/CV recommends protecting this program Review of SAF/IA records indicates that the Air Force operates three similar programs, all with country X, but each has unique areas of emphasis, and none provides the same access to partner R&D

Ops-to-Ops Staff Talks. The Air Force ops-to-ops staff talks were instituted in 2000 and defined in a guidance memo signed by the Vice Chief of Staff of the Air Force (AF/CV). The memo, entitled "International Engagement," specified seven countries with which the Air Force would conduct ops-to-ops talks, and tasked an Air Staff stakeholder (HQ AF/A5XX) to lead the program.[12] The ops-to-ops talks provide a good example of a stakeholder that can control the resources and has the authority to determine program objectives and can also identify a need and establish a program to satisfy that need. Exactly how that need is satisfied is a result of the design and theory of the program (i.e., how was it determined that staff talks might fill the need for staff interoperability?), a point that illustrates the highly connected nature of the various levels of analysis.

The ops-to-ops talks also illustrate that needs assessments are usually not a one-time activity for a program. Information garnered from various types of assessments, such as outcomes and effects, can let a decisionmaker know if the overall need is being met. For example, in staff talks, there is some flexibility in deciding which participating country to include or exclude, and the decision is typically made on recommendations from HQ AF/A5XX to the AF/CV. To begin with, the AF/CV identified the overall need for the program. However, as the program has unfolded there has been an ongoing needs assessment to determine with which air forces to partner. Since the talks began in 2000 with the original seven participating countries, talks with at least four countries have concluded and eight new countries have been added, growing the group to 11 by 2008.

The conclusion of staff talks with selected countries indicates that the relationship is maturing and that other, often more substantive, security cooperation activities can fill the gap when the staff talks are no longer needed. In assessment terms, this demonstrates how a stakeholder might look for other programs that produce the same benefits with the same partners. The question that HQ AF/A5XX should gather data to answer is *whether the demand for the program is growing, steady,*

---

[12] Australia, France, Germany, Israel, Japan, Russia, and Singapore.

or shrinking. This type of ongoing needs assessment can also enhance understanding of how well the stakeholder designed the program.

CJCS Exercise FLEXIBLE RESPONSE. Although organizations that do not manage a program are rarely in a position to conduct a needs assessment, they can sometimes influence the stakeholder that does have that role. FLEXIBLE RESPONSE 2008 provides one example of how this can be done. USAFE, while planning its participation in the EUCOM program, decided to go a step beyond the CPX nature of the exercise. Drawing on the existing exercise scenario, 3 AF's assessment office (3 AF/A9), with the support of the 3 AF Vice Commander, developed an internal USAFE exercise to be conducted during FLEXIBLE RESPONSE. The idea was to add realism by requiring that the 31st Fighter Wing at Aviano Air Base simulate a response to a simulated chemical attack. Much of this would include communicating with 3 AF and simulating the deployment of first responders and other follow-on actions to mitigate the consequences of the attack.

USAFE successfully completed the "Air Force–only" portion of the FLEXIBLE RESPONSE exercise in a way that was largely transparent to EUCOM and other participating units.[13] However, the lessons learned from this effort were collected and submitted to EUCOM (and the broader joint community) along with the lessons learned from the main exercise activity. Because these lessons learned are drawn on in the development of future iterations of the exercise, USAFE and 3 AF were able, in this way, to indirectly influence the needs assessment for the FLEXIBLE RESPONSE Exercise Program.

Canadian C-17 FMS Support Case. Air Force involvement in DCS cases is generally limited to ensuring that the sale complies with U.S. law. This means that the Air Force has limited insight into how the foreign partner will use the equipment and limited influence over the type of equipment purchased. This lack of insight can be perceived by the Air Force as a gap, or a need, that should be filled. To fill this gap (partially, at least), the Air Force can use persuasion to influence the decisions of foreign air forces and other non–Air Force stakeholders by suggesting an attractive FMS support case, for example.

---

[13] Discussion with USAFE official, July 2008.

This is precisely what the Air Force did with the Canadian C-17 sale, which enabled the Air Force to work closely with the Canadians on training, maintenance, sustainment, and operational issues related to the employment of the aircraft. In this case, the 516 AESG was able to leverage the C-17 GSP contract to develop an attractive companion FMS case for the Canadians.

This FMS case is discussed in greater detail in the next section, but there is one aspect of that case that is inextricably linked to the DCS. The 516 AESG was aware that many of the items that would go into the production of the Canadian aircraft, although technically not part of the DCS case, were already available as spare parts under the GSP. By providing a number of items back to Boeing as government-furnished equipment, the overall cost of the DCS could be reduced. Canada agreed, and in conjunction with the DCS case, an FMS case was initiated that included the purchase of spare parts and production items from the U.S. Air Force.[14] The parts were then transferred from the 516 AESG to Boeing and used in the production of the four Canadian C-17s.[15] As a result of this effort, the Air Force was able to gain insight into the needs of the Canadians in their acquisition of the C-17s via FMS.

Level 2: Design and Theory

This section continues with the description of the same three Air Force security cooperation programs, focusing this time on how the key stakeholders develop the theory and design of the programs. The team found that the number of stakeholders engaged at this level increased dramatically for both the ops-to-ops staff talks and the FMS case. Some of this additional involvement is the result of needing to bring in subject matter expertise, for example, to review an agenda or an exercise scenario. In the FMS case, the requirement for additional stakeholders

---

[14] Discussion with 516 AESG and AFSAC officials, July 2008.

[15] This included 18 engines plus 80–100 additional items, including defensive systems such as the Large Aircraft Infrared Countermeasures system, global positioning system equipment, flares, classified communications security (COMSEC) equipment, ground support equipment, and palletized seating.

is more formal and is governed by the directives that prescribe how an FMS case should be developed. Table 4.3 shows the stakeholders and the associated assessment questions.

Ops-to-Ops Staff Talks. Air Force–managed programs offer a good example of how a key stakeholder can design a program to fill a perceived gap. The main objective of Air Force staff talks is to increase staff interoperability with select partner nations, which in turn can be linked to the SAF/IA-developed AFGPS end state of building, sustaining, and expanding international relationships that are critical enablers for the Expeditionary Air and Space Force. From a SAF/IA perspective, the theory behind the AFGPS is to establish a critical link between national-level strategy and policy to Air Force planning. Looking at the theory behind the staff talks, we can see that the question being asked during the needs assessment was, "How do we increase interoperability among the staffs?" The underlying assumption is that the ops-to-ops talks will meet the need for increasing staff interoperability, thus enhancing the relationships with the partner air forces.

Designing the staff talks entails the development of agendas, an activity analogous to setting output objectives for the program. In other words, the HQ AF/A5XX action officers make decisions about what topics might further the overall program objective, an activity that could be assessed by the first of the generic assessment questions, "Does logic lead us to expect that, given the inputs to the program, we should see the outputs claimed for the program?" To do this, HQ AF/A5XX solicits agenda inputs from the affected COCOM, MAJCOM, SAF/IA, the Air Staff, and the partner country five to six months before an event. Agenda inputs form the basis for the discussions and are typically related to issues that can enhance the interoperability of the staffs. Other discussion items typically include related security cooperation programs, such as the Air Force MPEP, training, and exercises. Once the agendas are completed, HQ AF/A5XX requests approval from the A3/A5.

CJCS Exercise FLEXIBLE RESPONSE. USAFE participation in EUCOM's FLEXIBLE RESPONSE exercise also provides an example of how the Air Force can help a non–Air Force stakeholder design a program. The exercise consisted of several simulated incidents at various

Table 4.3
Stakeholders and Assessment Questions for Design and Theory of a Program

Program	Stakeholders	Assessment Question	Illustrative Answer
Ops-to-ops staff talks	HQ AF/A5XX Air Component Commands Deputy Chief of Staff, Operations, Plans, and Requirements, Headquarters Air Force (A3/A5) Other Air Staff offices SAF/IA	Does logic lead us to expect that, given the inputs to the program, we should see the outputs claimed for the program? Do assumptions linking program performance to security cooperation focus areas appear logical?	Trip reports, program agreements, and anecdotal interactions with partner air forces confirm the logic Analysis of key assumptions and cause-effect relationships within them confirms the program's design and theory logic
CJCS Exercise FLEXIBLE RESPONSE	USAFE 3 AF 86 AW	Do the claimed associations between security cooperation focus areas and regional/functional end states seem logically consistent? Have previous efforts like this realized the desired outcomes?	Analysis of after-action and end-of-tour reports, and periodic program reporting for 1993–2003 concerning 45 efforts revealed mixed outcomes; only 20 percent reported increased partner aviation capabilities, and 70 percent improved relations and trust
Canadian C-17 FMS support case	516 AESG SAF/IA HQ AMC AFSAC HQ AETC/IA AFSAT Headquarters AETC Directorate of Intelligence and Air, Space and Information Operations (HQ AETC/A2/A3) 19 AF 373 TRS 373 TRS Detachment 5	Has the program produced desired outputs or outcomes in the past?	Analysis of reports (see above) for 2004–2006 reflects improvements over earlier efforts: 28 percent improved interoperability, 30 percent reduced fears about allowing Air Force permission to base forces at partner airfields

locations, all occurring within a relatively compressed period of time. At Landstuhl Air Base, Germany, the exercise participants responded to a scenario involving a radiological dispersal device; high explosives were detonated at Vogelweh Air Base several miles to the east; and further south in the Bavarian Alps, an outbreak of plague was unleashed at Garmisch, home to the DoD George C. Marshall European Center for Security Studies. In Italy, Aviano Air Base was attacked with chemical weapons. As discussed above, responses to these simulated incidents were for the most part simply "talked through" by senior leaders at USAFE and 3 AF. This reveals the theory that discussing which procedures to implement and how, in a realistic setting, can be useful in increasing readiness to respond to an actual incident. Moreover, by working with partner countries, in this case Germany and Italy, the exercise is designed to address disaster response and consequence management security cooperation objectives. From an assessment standpoint, this is an area in which the *associations between security cooperation focus areas and regional/functional end states could be examined.* To validate this theory, stakeholders might gather data from the exercises to determine whether the assumptions linking program performance (i.e., increased readiness to respond to an emergency) to the security cooperation focus area (i.e., an exercise) appear logical. The obvious limitation is that the procedures are not actually exercised, and the first responders may or may not benefit from the discussions. But CPXs can demonstrate that the senior leaders are familiar with the procedures and the decisions they might be called on to make under pressure. They also test command and control systems and, in the case of FLEXIBLE RESPONSE, the adequacy of cross-service agreements. Finally, they perform a role analogous to the proposed "design and theory" assessment itself. CPXs can enable stakeholders to determine if capabilities are adequate, even if present to the degree postulated.

FLEXIBLE RESPONSE planners acknowledged the limitations of the CPX and decided that actually executing the emergency response procedures might demonstrate whether they would work.[16] Accordingly, the exercise scenarios were developed with an added "live" ele-

---

[16] Discussions with EUCOM and USAFE officials, June 2008.

ment, one that would include first responders actually demonstrating their ability to execute the procedures. USAFE and EUCOM planners elected to use the Landstuhl radiological dispersal device scenario to exercise elements of an agreement between the United States and Germany, affecting disaster response at Ramstein Air Base and the former Landstuhl Air Base. Landstuhl, currently home to the Army's Regional Medical Center, has no first-response capability of its own and is serviced instead through an agreement with the 86th Airlift Wing at Ramstein Air Base and local German first responders. In this way, planners would be able to demonstrate the actual execution of procedures for responding to the attack, including the support agreement that had been developed between the United States and Germany.

Canadian C-17 FMS Support Case. The theory behind the Canadian C-17 FMS case conforms largely to directives established by non–Air Force stakeholders. Despite this, there was considerable room for Air Force stakeholders to theorize and make decisions about the design of the program. Because the program had multiple facets, a number of Air Force stakeholders were involved. As described above, the 516 AESG is the SPO responsible for acquisition and sustainment of the Air Force's C-17 transport aircraft. In addition, the group manages C-17–related security assistance cases and is the primary stakeholder in the portion of the case that deals with equipment transfer.

The primary tool used by the group is the GSP contract with Boeing. Under this contract, Boeing performs some functions traditionally done by Air Force organizations, such as managing the supply chain for all parts and spares that are unique to the C-17. To use the GSP to support the Canadian C-17 sales case, the 516th's Canada IPT prepared an amendment to the contract, approved by AFSAC, which specified exactly which services Boeing would provide. This arrangement suggests two things:

- The planners believed that the best way to meet the objectives was to define them contractually with a private sector entity.
- It would be more efficient to use the existing contract rather than negotiating a new one.

In terms of design and theory, this is an example of how planners draw on past experience to develop new programs. In this case, the right assessment question was, *"Have previous instances of this kind of effort realized the desired outcomes?"* or perhaps, *"Has the program produced desired outputs or outcomes in the past?"* Asking these questions allows planners to avoid potential pitfalls and make informed decisions about the best way to proceed.

In some instances, creative ways are needed to solve problems outside the scope of the GSP contract. For example, when an item of ground support equipment (a heavy forklift loader) was unavailable to support the case, the 516 AESG identified the problem and SAF/IA then arranged to have the Air Force lease ground support equipment to the Canadian government. The item was designed specifically for use with the C-17 but was no longer available commercially. By working with AMC, SAF/IA was able to lease two of its loaders for two years.

On the training side of the FMS case, AFSAT coordinated with AETC and with the Canadian armed forces to establish objectives for the training. At AETC, AFSAT coordinated with 19th Air Force to develop the flying training curriculum and with HQ Air Education and Training Command, Space and Information Operations (AETC/A3) to develop the technical training curriculum.[17] The flying training, as it turns out, is essentially the same as that provided to U.S. Air Force C-17 crew members. For the technical training, AETC officials, including the technical training manager from the 37th Training Wing at Sheppard Air Force Base, Texas, participated in a number of planning meetings organized by AFSAT. These meetings also included Canadian participants. These meetings enabled training managers and subject matter experts to develop course objectives for a proposed course of instruction, identify the locations and materials required, and prepare schedules for the courses.[18]

Part of this effort included modifying the U.S. curriculum to fit the Canadian concept for maintaining the aircraft. Although the

---

[17]   Discussions with AFSAT and AETC officials, July 2008.

[18]   Travel expenses for participation in these meetings were funded by the FMS case. Discussion with AETC official, June 2008.

United States trains seven separate specialties for C-17 maintenance, the Canadians had decided to consolidate those specialties to just two: avionics specialists and mechanics specialists. This decision required that the U.S. curriculum be consolidated in a corresponding way.

When considering the theory behind this course of action, it seems reasonable to assume that planners made two assumptions, most likely based on past experience: first, that U.S. Air Force training methods would be adequate for the Canadian aircrew members and maintenance technicians and, second, that some modifications to the standard U.S. Air Force training courses might be necessary to conform to Canadian operating concepts. Thus, it was essential to include the Canadians in the process from the very beginning.

Another design and theory decision is illustrated by AFSAT, AETC, and AMC efforts to incorporate "seasoning" training for the Canadians. This type of training is based on the theory that working on the job with an experienced mechanic would increase new technicians' proficiency. In addition, as the number of qualified and experienced C-17 technicians in the Royal Canadian Air Force grows, the seasoning training can shift from AMC to the Canadian base at Trenton, Ontario. Similarly, over time, the responsibility for instructing some elements of the technical training course is being shifted from Detachment 5 to the Canadian Air Force, allowing the U.S. Air Force to shorten the training course.

Level 3: Process and Implementation

This section describes some of the major processes undertaken by stakeholders during the implementation of a program. As shown in Table 4.4, these activities can include preparing for an event, such as an ops-to-ops talk, securing resources for an activity, resolving problems, and conducting training. For Air Force–managed programs, Air Force stakeholders control the implementation from beginning to end and have a great deal of flexibility in determining the issues and topics that are covered. During ops-to-ops talks, for example, the U.S. Air Force and foreign air force delegations agree on the agenda but also typically discuss other security cooperation programs. These discussions

Table 4.4
Stakeholders and Assessment Questions for Process and Implementation

Program	Stakeholder	Assessment Question	Illustrative Answer
Ops-to-ops staff talks	HQ AF/A5XX AF/A3/A5	Is the program resourced sufficiently to perform its functions and activities relative to demand for them?	COCOM IPRs have identified funding shortfalls for 2003–2007 as a constraint; partner requests consistently exceed program resources
CJCS FLEXIBLE RESPONSE	USAFE 3 AF/A3XJ 3 AF/A9		
Canadian C-17 FMS support case	516 AESG SAF/IA AFSAC AFSAT 373 TRS Detachment 5 Headquarters Air Force Operational Training Division (HQ AF/A3O-AT) HQ AMC	Does the program meet deadlines, fill quotas, and otherwise satisfy performance and administrative standards?	A review of IG inspection reports, program security plans, delegation of disclosure authority letters, and similar documentation indicates that the program meets its performance and regulatory requirements
		Does the program observe restrictions and prohibitions?	
		Does the program accommodate the transfer of technology?	A review of IG inspection reports, program security plans, delegation of disclosure authority letters, and similar documentation indicates that the program complies with its appropriate restrictions and prohibitions
		What are the authorities attached to the resources?	
		Is program execution conducted so as to foster positive impressions of it among its participants?	Feedback from participants in 2006–2007, as captured in after-action reports, project reports, requests to participate, numbers of nominations, and exit surveys, indicates that positive impressions grew 8 percent over the period 2004–2005

can provide insight into the partner air forces' views on military personnel exchanges, exercises, and even FMS or IMET training in which they are involved. The talks also offer an opportunity to build on the relationship between the two air forces, often through social events and interaction between the officers. These types of informal interactions offer opportunities for stakeholders to gather data that can potentially answer *whether or not the program is fostering a positive impression among the participants.* These opportunities are often easy to miss, as they are not always part of the formal program.

Ops-to-Ops Staff Talks. To implement security cooperation programs, as described in Chapter Two, the Air Force either controls funding and manpower resources or receives those resources from a third party. In the case of a program that uses Air Force–controlled resources, AFIs typically describe processes for their use. To illustrate, Air Force ops-to-ops staff talks and the Air Force MPEP both use Air Force O&M funds as the major resource for implementing the programs. For ops-to-ops staff talks, the funds are centrally maintained at the A3/A5 level through the normal O&M budget. Headquarters AF/A5XX requests funding case by case, meaning that funding is allocated only as needed. In general, O&M funds cover travel expenses for the general officer heading the delegation and for one action officer from Headquarters AF/A5XX; depending on the agenda, the funds will also cover the travel costs for one or two subject matter experts. All other participants, including those representing the partner countries, must cover their own expenses. HQ AF/A5XX draws on official representation funds (ORFs) to pay for mementos and a portion of dining and entertainment expenses, in addition to travel.[19] In other words, there is no unique source of funding for the staff talks or MPEP.

The Air Force has several ways to assess how well it complies with the restrictions and prohibitions on the expenditure of funds for security cooperation programs. AFIs provide specific requirements for assessing the use of these resources, including both how the resources were used and whether their use was cost-effective. The assessments are typically accomplished by a third party organization within the Air Force, such as the Air Force Inspection Agency or the AFAA. This information, in turn, can be fed into ongoing needs assessments. Thus, AFI 65-603 not only describes how ORF will be used but also directs the AFAA to conduct yearly audits of the expenditures.[20] Similarly, AFI 65-201 requires the establishment of internal controls to ensure

---

[19] The use of these funds is governed by U.S. Air Force, *Official Representation Funds— Guidance and Procedures*, AFI 65-603, February 17, 2004c.

[20] U.S. Air Force, 2004c, p. 9.

that resources, such as Air Force O&M funds, are properly handled.[21] In addition, the Air Force IG routinely conducts inspections to ensure that mission areas, such as financial management, comptroller, and contracting, comply with applicable laws and directives.

CJCS Exercise FLEXIBLE RESPONSE. Other programs that the Air Force supports rely largely on resources provided by a third party. An example of this is the Air Force's participation in a CJCS exercise. Typically, participation in planning conferences for the exercise is funded by the Joint Staff, as are many expenses associated with conducting the exercise, such as flying hours and the actual participation of Air Force personnel. Other expenses, such as the cost of lodging, per diems, and contract support, are budgeted for by the Air Force and are part of the service's O&M funds.

In a CPX such as FLEXIBLE RESPONSE, the primary Air Force resource used is manpower—essentially the time and effort that the assigned airmen contribute—meaning that Joint Staff exercise funds were used to largely reimburse USAFE's participation costs. In such situations, USAFE should collect data to assess whether its participation is *resourced sufficiently to perform the functions and activities requested* by EUCOM.

The "live" portion of the exercise, as described above, required that both U.S. and German first responders work together at Landstuhl Air Base to demonstrate the provisions of the first-response agreement between the two countries. Although the resources used for the "Air Force–only" exercise between Aviano Air Base and 3 AF were also primarily manpower, Air Force O&M funds were the sole resource used, with no reimbursement from the Joint Staff.

In exercises such as FLEXIBLE RESPONSE, the Air Force has learned that careful planning is the key to effective implementation. In the months leading up to FLEXIBLE RESPONSE, Air Force stakeholders, particularly USAFE (as the air component command to EUCOM) participated in planning conferences to help develop the exercise scenarios and objectives. USAFE's participation in exercises, including such combined exercises as FLEXIBLE RESPONSE, is

---

[21] U.S. Air Force, *Managers' Internal Control Program Procedures,* AFI 65-201, 2006e.

guided by AFI 10-204.[22] Although USAFE assigns primary responsibility for planning and oversight of this participation to HQ USAFE/A3XJ, much of the actual planning and development of the exercise is conducted by 3 AF/A9.

Assessments of CJCS exercises may be conducted using the routine procedures prescribed by Chairman of the Joint Chiefs of Staff Manual (CJCSM) 3500.03 and Chairman of the Joint Chiefs of Staff Instruction (CJCSI) 3150.05.[23] The procedures require that COCOMs nominate a representative sample of exercises for assessment each year.

In addition, lessons learned are provided routinely using the procedures prescribed in CJCSI 3150.25.[24] These procedures require that the COCOMs submit lessons learned from exercises and other training activities in a standardized way so that they can be used to inform the development of future similar exercises, among other things. USAFE participates in this process. Interestingly, even though EUCOM was not involved in the Air Force–only exercise between Aviano Air Base and 3 AF, the lessons learned from that exercise were forwarded to EUCOM along with the main FLEXIBLE RESPONSE lessons learned, making them available to planners of future exercises. Again, this illustrates the interconnected nature of the levels of analysis, since by using these lessons learned, the exercise planners will be able to assess the effectiveness of their original design and theory.

Canadian C-17 FMS Support Case. As was true for this case at the first two levels of assessment, the Air Force also can manage complex activities in support of non–Air Force stakeholders.

To ensure that direct commercial and FMS are consistent with U.S. laws governing the transfer of military articles to foreign countries, private corporations must first obtain an export license from the

---

[22] U.S. Air Force, undated-b. The term *combined* refers to military activity involving both the United States and foreign militaries.

[23] Chairman of the Joint Chiefs of Staff, *Joint Training Manual for the Armed Forces of the United States,* Manual 3500.03, Washington, D.C., undated-a; Chairman of the Joint Chiefs of Staff, *Assessment Program,* Instruction 3150.05, Washington, D.C., undated-b.

[24] Chairman of the Joint Chiefs of Staff, *Joint Lessons Learned Program,* Instruction 3150.25, Washington, D.C., undated-c.

U.S. government. Although such stakeholders as SAF/IA and AFSAC expend some effort conducting these technical transfer compliance reviews, the Air Force is subsequently not directly involved in support at all levels of a DCS case.[25] Nonetheless, the Air Force does have a role in assessment here, at a minimum *to understand if restrictions and prohibitions regarding technical transfers have been observed.*

This is unlike an FMS case, in which the Air Force can engage directly with the foreign air force to set output objectives and design activities to implement the program. The lack of involvement in DCS cases results in a lack of Air Force insight into how the equipment will be used by the foreign air force. In short, the direct commercial sale may or may not further progress toward objectives that are important to the Air Force, such as relationship-building and interoperability, the way an FMS case can.

It is possible, though, for the Air Force to influence decisions made about security assistance. As mentioned above, in the case of the DCS transfer of four C-17s to the Canadian Royal Air Force, the Air Force recognized the benefits of building on the U.S.-Canada relationship and fostering interoperability between the Canadian and U.S. C-17 fleets. The 516 AESG understood the details of the DCS case and developed an approach that allowed it to effectively link a large FMS support and training case to it. As a result, even though there is no direct Air Force activity in the DCS case, the FMS case gave the Air Force a way to gain insight into the overall effectiveness of the Canadian C-17 sale.

As with the DCS case, at the beginning of an FMS case, SAF/IA performs functions that help ensure compliance with U.S. laws regarding the transfer of military equipment. However, the case itself is largely developed externally by AFSAC case managers who are called on for expertise in Air Force systems. In this particular case, AFSAC personnel worked closely with AFSAT, AETC, AMC, and others to

---

[25] This may include reviews to ensure that the sale is compliant with the Arms Export Control Act or the Missile Technology Control Regime and, for the purposes of assessment, for example, stakeholders should gather data regarding these reviews to assess how well the Air Force observes restrictions and prohibitions on technical transfer.

finalize the support and training case. In this way, Air Force security assistance planners gain insight into the case requirements and begin to understand how the case might tie into Air Force security cooperation objectives.

Air Force stakeholders (i.e., SAF/IA, AETC, the 516 AESG, and AFSAC) with positions that directly support the Canadian C-17 program are reimbursed through the FMS case.[26]

The day-to-day execution of the C-17 FMS support case is generally managed by the 516 AESG, with a relatively low level of involvement by AFSAC. This is because AFSAC case managers typically manage supplies and parts that are common across multiple systems, or in some cases they manage older, more established systems, such as the F-16. Accordingly, AFSAC personnel have sometimes helped the 516 AESG obtain parts or supplies that are not unique to the C-17.

Another example of interaction between the 516th and AFSAC is the modification of contracts. Although the 516th has a contracting officer assigned, modifications to contracts are reviewed and approved by personnel at AFSAC. When the case ends in 2012, it is expected that the management of many aspects of the follow-on case will be transitioned to AFSAC case managers. This is typical and reflects the maturation of the system and the increasing commonality of its parts with those of other systems.[27] Thus, it is important for both AFSAC and the 516 AESG to consider assessment questions regarding *the program's ability to meet deadlines, fill quotas, and otherwise satisfy performance and administrative standards.*

The Air Force also has a number of roles associated with training in this case. First, AFSAT serves as the "face to the customer," taking proposals for the conduct of training to the Canadians and serving as the interlocutor between the Canadians and the U.S. trainers and subject matter experts. SAF/IA also is engaged with the training pro-

---

[26] The costs of FMS training, for example, are documented and provided to the Deputy Assistant Secretary for Budget to ensure accurate financial reporting. See U.S. Air Force, *Dedicated Foreign Military Sales Training Programs,* AFI 65-607, 1997a.

[27] The case was established in 2007 and will close in 2012. One example given by a 516 AESG official was that if the follow-on air refueling aircraft were produced by Boeing, then there would likely be a number of parts in common with the C-17.

gram implementation but focuses on activities that are more "high-level" than is the day-to-day case management. These activities can include the preparation of agreements, leases, and other arrangements that help to facilitate the execution of the case. One example is the process for allocating flying training slots for international partners. AFSAT, in coordination with SAF/IA and HQ AF/A3OT (Operations Training), conducts an International Flying Training Board that prioritizes the requests for flying training. In this process, SAF/IA makes the final decision as to which countries will get the available flying training slots. SAF/IA, therefore, might be concerned with assessments of *how well the program is resourced to perform its functions and activities relative to demand for them.*

The day-to-day management of the training is generally the responsibility of AETC and its subordinate units. Detachment 5 of the 373 TRS was selected for the training because of the training resources already at its disposal, including a number of training devices, such as engines and other major aircraft components, as well as mock-ups of aircraft systems.[28] To ensure that the detachment had the right mix of skills to conduct the training, AETC arranged to have instructors from other bases reassigned to Charleston Air Force Base to augment the unit's expertise. Some of these instructors were permanently assigned. However, a number of additional instructors were assigned only temporarily and returned to their home bases after the program was firmly established. As the detachment at Charleston began preparing for its role as the primary unit for training Canadian C-17 technicians, the training detachment at McChord Air Force Base, Washington, which had previously trained Australian C-17 maintenance technicians in a separate sales case, briefly provided some of the expertise and initial training for the Canadians.[29] With the Detachment 5 program fully under way, the throughput of students is approximately six avionics technicians and six mechanics per year. The training of the Canadian

---

[28] These training devices were purchased by AMC for AETC to use during training of AMC C-17 maintenance technicians.

[29] Two AETC field training detachments are collocated with operational U.S. Air Force C-17 units. Discussion with AETC officials, July 2008.

students became AETC's first priority, even ahead of the AMC personnel assigned to the U.S. Air Force C-17 unit.[30]

In terms of assessment, AETC stakeholders should be routinely gathering data to assess *whether the program meets its deadlines, fills quotas, and otherwise satisfies performance and administrative standards.*

Process-wise, the training activities are documented using standard AETC processes, and those successfully finishing the technical training program receive a certificate of completion. Once the Canadian technicians completed the AETC course, they remained at Charleston Air Force Base to work under the supervision of U.S. C-17 maintenance technicians assigned to the operational C-17 unit. This allowed them to get hands-on experience under the mentorship of veteran technicians. To ensure that this on-the-job training (OJT) would meet Canadian requirements, AFSAT and AETC training managers met with counterparts from HQ AMC to develop the program and decide on its structure. This "seasoning" training is documented by the OJT supervisor in a ledger maintained by the trainee.

Not all of the required training for the Canadian crews and maintenance technicians was done by AETC, despite its lead role. After coordinating with personnel at AFSAT, the 516 AESG confirmed that the operation and maintenance of some items could not be included in the flying training or technical training conducted by AETC. As a result, the 516 AESG arranged for the training to take place through a variety of other sources. For example, it coordinated with the Army to provide training on the Automated Air Load Planning System (AALPS), which is used to calculate the best way to load personnel and equipment onto a transport aircraft. Because the Army is a major user of Air Force airlift capability, AALPS is managed by the U.S. Army's Transportation Information Systems PMO. As a result, the 516 AESG arranged for the Army to deploy a team to Trenton to train the Royal Canadian Air Force aircrew and ground support personnel to use the system.

---

[30] U.S. Air Force, *Training Development, Delivery, and Evaluation,* AFI 36-2201, Vol. 1, Table A5.1, 2002, provided the guidance that gave the international students top priority.

Level 4: Outcomes and Effects

At the fourth level of assessment, the number of key stakeholders engaged begins to tail off, as depicted in Table 4.5. For the most part, this reflects the fact that outcomes are primarily the concern of the higher-level organizations or commands. Despite that, there is a need for input from lower-level stakeholders, including such organizations as

Table 4.5
Stakeholders and Questions for Assessing Outcomes and Effects

Program	Stakeholder	Assessment Question	Illustrative Answer
Ops-to-ops staff talks	AF/A3/A5 HQ AF/A5XX	Do participants leave with more skill/ capability than they arrived with?	According to participant entry and exit testing from 2006–2008, 15 percent of participants from EUCOM AOR improved, 4 percent from CENTCOM AOR improved, and 8 percent from PACOM AOR improved
CJCS Exercise FLEXIBLE RESPONSE	USAFE 3 AF	Is partner capability in the program's areas growing, stable, or declining?	
Canadian C-17 FMS support case	SAF/IA HQ AETC/IA AFSAT AFSAC 516 AESG HQ AMC	Is the program's contribution to other security cooperation efforts growing, stable, or declining?	Alumni data collected by the program office indicate that 40 percent of graduates from 2006–2007 have retired, for a net decline in capacity; 74 percent of UK Royal Air Force graduates remain in active service, for a net increase in capabilities; and 4 percent of Spanish pilots retired, leaving the number of NATO-interoperable aircrews stable
			12 percent growth in a partner country's participation in the program from 2006–2008 correlates with the Ministry of Defence (MOD) decision to buy F-16s and to make a number of air bases available for Air Force tankers ISR

HQ AF/A5XP, 3 AF, 516 AESG, and AFSAC, which provide information to A3/A5, USAFE, and SAF/IA.

Ops-to-Ops Staff Talks. Determining the outcomes and effects of programs for which the Air Force sets the objectives can be relatively straightforward and, as will be discussed in Chapter Five, indeed should be an Air Force responsibility. For example, after every Air Force ops-to-ops staff talk, HQ AF/A5XX prepares a summary report that is routed to the CSAF and SAF for review. In addition, HQ AF/A5XX provides a monthly update to A3/A5 regarding the status of any action items that resulted from the various staff talks. This is part of the process and implementation for the staff talks, but it may also serve a variety of other purposes: to validate the design and theory and to feed into the ongoing needs assessment. Finally, as action items are closed, the evidence that staff interoperability is being achieved may indicate that an outcome has been achieved.

Assessing and identifying the outcomes from staff talks might be as simple as receiving information from a partner air force staff member on a topic previously discussed during the talks. This evidence of enhanced interoperability between the Air Staff and a partner air force's staff differs from the output of an agenda item as explained above. For example, if the partner air force submits a request for assistance in the future, and it uses the format and all of the information described at the previous ops-to-ops talks, this might be evidence that the desired outcome has been achieved. As a minimum, it would validate the design and theory of the agenda that guided the talks and, from an assessment standpoint, this kind of information would be useful in helping stakeholders understand if the partner's capabilities in the program's areas are growing, stable, or declining.

CJCS Exercise FLEXIBLE RESPONSE. Gathering information about specific security cooperation activities is important but so is dissemination of that information. Sometimes, what a program manager may view as an output from an activity can actually be considered an outcome by another program manager. This was the case with USAFE's participation in FLEXIBLE RESPONSE. Because USAFE does not set the overall objectives for the exercise (EUCOM does), USAFE is not in an ideal position to assess whether the exercise's outcomes were achieved. However, USAFE has a role in assessing whether outputs were achieved, particularly those that it incorporated into the exercise design during the exercise planning phase. One such output objective was to exercise the agreement with the German government on cooperation with and sharing of first-response capabilities. As mentioned above, this output was achieved but, interestingly, this same success can also be viewed as an outcome in the eyes of the USAFE representatives who negotiated the agreement. These types of data could be useful to stakeholders as they try to understand *whether their program's contribution to other security cooperation efforts is growing, stable, or declining.*

Canadian C-17 FMS Support Case. The Air Force is even further removed from the process of deciding outcome objectives for security assistance programs, but the Air Force can and does influence those decisions. Moreover, the Air Force can also set its own outcome objectives for an FMS case, such as interoperability or relationship-building. Because these outcomes are not a formal part of the sales case, measuring them is solely an Air Force responsibility. In the case of Canadian C-17 support and training, for example, personnel from Canada's Air Force Headquarters in Winnipeg, Manitoba, periodically meet with AETC, AFSAT, and AMC personnel to review the program's progress. This forum not only allows the U.S. Air Force to discuss issues of interest, but also lets the Royal Canadian Air Force provide feedback regarding the quality of the training from their perspective.[31] In this way, the Air Force can hear firsthand whether the desired outcomes are being achieved. These reviews are an example of the Air Force stakeholders' attempts to understand if *the program's participants leave with more skill and capability than they started with.* Finally, as a matter of standard AETC practice, the entire course is reviewed every two years to determine if it is still meeting its objectives. The effort enabled the Canadians to take their C-17s into theater as planned.

Assessment of equipment transfer activities are accomplished primarily by the 516 AESG through its quality assurance surveillance of the GSP contract. In addition, AFSAC reviews all major FMS programs semiannually. This review, known as the International Acquisi-

---

[31] Discussion with AFMC official, July 2008.

tion, Sustainment, and Training Review, draws on relevant data from the various contract surveillance plans and the assessment process-oriented activities, such as the timeliness of case closure at the end of a case.[32] These data are then summarized in a series of charts that indicate the relative status of the program.

Level 5: Cost-Effectiveness

In the case studies examined, processes are in place to examine the use of resources, but there is no focused effort to assess the cases' overall cost-effectiveness. There is an obvious need for this type of assessment for programs that are directly owned by the Air Force, such as the ops-to-ops talks, UNIFIED ENGAGEMENT seminars, and MPEP. These programs could indeed benefit from cost-effectiveness assessment using questions such as those shown in Table 4.6.

Although Air Force–appropriated funds are not used to develop or execute FMS cases, Air Force stakeholders could evaluate the cost-effectiveness of the program to reduce costs and ensure that the customer is satisfied with the value received. Better cost analysis would also help in FMS budget requests, especially for new programs such as international C-17 sales and, eventually, Joint Strike Fighter FMS cases.

A number of efforts within the Air Force draw on financial data to assess how well Air Force programs are managed, and to some degree each assesses the cost-effectiveness of these programs. These include activities conducted by the Air Force IG (and the MAJCOM inspector generals), the AFAA, HQ AF/A9AO (Analysis and Assessments), and the Air Force corporate structure (AFCS), which reviews programmatic issues and makes decisions regarding Air Force resources.[33] Although these efforts touch on aspects of Air Force security cooperation, none are aimed at assessing security cooperation as a whole.

---

[32] Participants in the International Acquisition Sustainment and Training Review include AFSAC, the SPO, SAF/IA, AETC/IA, and AFSAT.

[33] The AFCS draws on Air Staff and secretariat officials to work through programming issues.

Table 4.6
Cost-Effectiveness Assessment Questions

Program	Stakeholder	Assessment Question	Illustrative Answer
Ops-to-ops staff talks	HQ AF/A3/A5	How do cost-effectiveness data compare with other security cooperation programs?	Participation hastens partner adoption of Air Force tactics, techniques, and procedures.
CJCS Exercise FLEXIBLE RESPONSE	None	What is the program's ROI?	After participating in the last exercise, MOD announced that it would support U.S. contingencies in the region with its air expeditionary wing squadron.
Canadian C-17 FMS support case	HQ AMC HQ AETC AFSAC	How does the ROI compare with that of other Air Force programs?	
		Do any other Air Force programs produce the same outputs for less money?	
		What can be done to reduce the cost per unit of output?	

In one case, the financial management aspects of security cooperation activities are indirectly assessed but only as a part of the larger Air Force program of financial management assessment. For example, AFSAC's financial management activities are documented and then assessed by the AFMC IG. This is part of the Air Force's effort to implement the Federal Manager's Financial Integrity Act, in which Air Force organizations are required to develop internal controls to ensure that programs are being effectively and efficiently carried out.[34] The AFMC IG, in turn, conducts an annual compliance inspection of AFSAC's internal controls but only to ensure that the controls are properly implemented.[35] This is different from assessing the cost-effectiveness of AFSAC's activities, however.

Similarly, the expenditure of ORFs that are used to support ops-to-ops staff talks and Air Force UNIFIED ENGAGEMENT semi-

---

[34] U.S. Air Force, 2006e.

[35] MAJCOMs typically conduct compliance inspections for subordinate units. AFMC, for example, conducts recurring compliance inspection of AFSAC, to include its manager's internal control program. In addition, the AFMC IG considers how well AFSAC and the other product centers are complying with other AFIs.

nars are audited annually. However, this annual audit looks at all ORF expenditures in the aggregate and does not attempt to single out and assess just the expenditures related to security cooperation. We also found that expenditures for FMS training are reported routinely to the Office of the Assistant Secretary of the Air Force for Financial Management (SAF/FM), which in turn analyzes the data. However, SAF/FM is primarily interested in ensuring that the funds are being spent as programmed and that the Air Force is accurately reimbursed by the FMS case. The point is that none of these efforts consider the actual cost-effectiveness of Air Force security cooperation programs.

In 2003, DoD added "execution" to its planning, programming, and budgeting system. The new process, known as the PPBE Program, is designed to evaluate spending (the "execution" part) as a way to "determine how well the desired capabilities [have been] achieved."[36] The PPBE Program is implemented by the AFCS, which consists of a set of four, tiered organizations that review budgetary information and make decisions about what to include in the Air Force's annual budget request. Clearly, this process requires a great deal of prioritization and assessment regarding multiple programs' relative cost-effectiveness. At the top tier of the AFCS is the Air Force Council, which is chaired by the AF/CV and consists of the Air Force's top decisionmakers. SAF/IA is a member of the council. The two intermediate organizations, the Air Force Board and the Air Force Group, also have SAF/IA representation. At the lowest end of the AFCS are a set of panels chaired by offices across the Air Staff and the secretariat to represent the various Air Force missions and mission support areas.[37] According

---

[36] U.S. Air Force, *Control and Documentation of Air Force Programs,* AFI 16-501, August 15, 2006d, implements Management Initiative Decision (MID) 913 (Chairman of the Joint Chiefs of Staff, *Implementation of a 2-Year Planning, Programming, Budgeting and Execution Process,* May 22, 2003). According to this AFI, MID 913 "increased the effectiveness of AF Planning, Programming, and Budgeting and added additional emphasis to Execution."

[37] According to AFI 16-501 (CJCS, 2003), the mission panels include air superiority, global attack, information superiority, global mobility, and space superiority. Mission support panels include personnel and training, installation support, logistics, RDT&E, communications and information, special access required, national intelligence programs, competitive sourcing and privatization, and innovation.

to AFI 16-501, these panels are the "centers of expertise for their areas, and they are the first level of corporate deliberation in the AFCS."[38] *There is currently no panel for Air Force security cooperation and therefore no "center of expertise" within the AFCS to either conduct comprehensive cost-effectiveness assessments or advocate the inclusion of security cooperation programs in the PPBE Program.*

Conclusions

For each of the three programs described in this chapter, the study team found that multiple stakeholders are involved in each level of analysis, with the exception of cost-effectiveness. Moreover, in each instance, one primary stakeholder was involved in the four remaining levels: needs assessment, design and theory, process and implementation, and outcomes and effects.

Supporting stakeholders most often participate in the design and theory as well as the processes and implementation levels of analysis. This could be due to the primary stakeholder's need to bring in other stakeholders' expertise and resources during program development and execution. Table 4.7 summarizes the programs, the stakeholders, and the levels in which they are involved.

The study team also observed that the amount of formal guidance given to non–Air Force programs is much greater than that given to Air Force programs. For example, although AFM 16-101 (U.S. Air Force, 2003a) provides guidance for some Air Force security cooperation programs, it does not address all of them. Ops-to-ops staff talks, for example, are governed by an AF/CV memo, and UNIFIED ENGAGEMENT seminars have no formal guidance document at all. In contrast, participation in CJCS exercises is governed by AFI 10-204 (U.S. Air Force, undated), and some components, such as USAFE,

---

[38] CJCS, 2003, p. 9.

Table 4.7
Summary of Programs, Stakeholders, and Assessment Levels

	Needs Assessment	Design and Theory	Process and Implementation	Outcomes and Effects	Cost-Effectiveness
			Level of Analysis		
Operator-to-Operator Staff Talks					
AF/CV					
AF/A3/A5		√	√	√	√
SAF/IA		√			
HQ AF/A5XX	√	√	√	√	
Air Staff		√			
Components		√			
CJCS Exercise FLEXIBLE RESPONSE					
USAFE	√	√	√	√	
3 AF/CV	√				
3 AF/A9	√	√	√	√	
3 AF/A3XJ		√	√		
86 AW		√	√		
31 FW		√	√		
Canadian C-17 FMS Support Case					
SAF/IA	√	√	√	√	
HQ AMC		√	√	√	√
AFSAC	√	√	√	√	√
516 AESG	√	√	√	√	
HQ AF/A3OT			√		
HQ AETC/IA		√		√	√
AFSAT		√	√	√	
HQ AETC/A3		√			
19 AF		√			
373 TRS		√	√		

have developed their own detailed supplement to govern their participation in such activities as FLEXIBLE RESPONSE.

In the case of security assistance, Air Force stakeholders' activities are governed not only by such Air Force directives as AFM 16-101, and AFMC Instruction 16-101, but also by several non–Air Force directives, including DoD Manual 5105.38-M; DoD Financial Management Regulation 7000.14-R, Volume 15; and U.S.C. Title 22, §2761.[39]

Some Air Force organizations are not stakeholders involved in assessing some aspects of Air Force security cooperation programs. Specifically, the AFAA and the MAJCOM inspector generals assess stakeholders' use of "routine" Air Force processes that enable security cooperation activities. These assessments are essentially process and implementation assessments and focus on the appropriate use of resources and general compliance with directives and legal requirements. As a result, there is no need to create an additional assessment mechanism for these types of activities.

For most levels of analysis, stakeholders were conducting activities that could provide information to answer some of the generic assessment questions. However, not all of the questions could be associated with activities. For example, at the needs assessment level, the team was not able to identify a process that allowed stakeholders to understand the relative cost-effectiveness of comparable programs. This gap could affect how well any particular program might fare during budget cuts, when the overall importance of programs would be compared.

Moreover, cost-effectiveness assessments are not being conducted in a focused, comprehensive way. This is not to say that data that could contribute to such assessments are not being collected; in all likelihood, the financial reporting, after-action reporting, and lessons learned reporting are capturing much of the necessary information. What is missing is the process for analyzing that information to help Air Force leaders compare the various security cooperation programs to each other and to other Air Force programs. The AFCS, which includes SAF/IA,

---

[39] Air Force Materiel Command, "Foreign Military Sales Resources," AFMC Instruction 16-101, undated; U.S. Department of Defense, 2007; U.S. Department of Defense, "Security Assistance Policy and Procedures," undated-c.

could be one potential vehicle for this. It would require the inclusion of a security cooperation panel and the designation of an office to serve within the AFCS as the security cooperation "champion."

CHAPTER FIVE

Implementing a Comprehensive Assessment Framework

This chapter suggests a way for the Air Force to implement the comprehensive security cooperation assessment framework described in this monograph. The approach takes into account the different types of security cooperation programs in which the Air Force is involved, whether or not the Air Force is in charge; the different kinds of assessment that are possible and consistent with the intent of the GEF; the supporting/supported relationships that might be built to make such assessments possible; and the data that would have to be collected about specific security cooperation programs to conduct useful assessments. In the absence of a program directive giving specific responsibilities to the various stakeholders, using broad selection criteria can be useful in helping to think through the appropriate assessment roles of each stakeholder. We begin by describing the options.

Assessment Options

As noted above, the Air Force and the other military services have been assessing security cooperation activities for some time: evaluating exercises, surveying participants for their opinions about the value and utility of the activities, and inspecting units to assess the degree to which they adhere to the guidance and directives for carrying out these activities and actions.

To reiterate a point made above, conducting assessments is not new to the Air Force. Therefore, a goal might be to leverage the Air Force's existing capabilities to enable a more comprehensive approach to assessing security cooperation programs. As Chapter Four explained, assessments are not being conducted across all five levels of evaluation for all security cooperation programs, and assessments of cost-effectiveness were largely absent in the three cases that were examined.[1]

As explained in Chapter Three and illustrated in Chapter Four, the assessments of security cooperation programs should be consistent with the spirit of the instructions in the GEF and U.S. Air Force strategy. All of these programs have U.S. government stakeholders that are guided by specific authorities. Their authorities, which shape and influence their responsibilities, lead each stakeholder to a certain set of decisions that they may make about the program:

- whether it should continue
- whether it is well-conceived given the theory of how the program is supposed to help the Air Force, or other stakeholders, reach their respective goals and end states
- whether the process and implementation of the program are performing adequately or require revision
- whether the outcomes and effects of the program are meeting expectations
- whether the program is performing on a cost-benefit basis—delivering the expected "bang for the buck."

The type of assessment that stakeholders need depends on the specific decisions they expect to make about the program. Table 5.1 organizes these responsibility-assessment-decision relationships graphically. As noted in Chapter Three, assessment decisions at various levels should not be made in isolation. To a large extent, they should build on one another and draw from common sources of data. Furthermore, there should be a feedback loop in the hierarchy of assessment that permits stakeholders involved in assessing the need for a new or proposed program to make use of higher-level assessments conducted on related

---

[1] It is probably unrealistic to expect cost-effectiveness assessments when output/outcome cannot be measured in quantitative terms.

Table 5.1
Responsibility-Assessment-Decision Relationships

Need for the Program	Design and Theory	Process and Implementation	Outcomes and Effects	Cost-Effectiveness
Goals: Relationships				
Capability				
U.S. access to partner country COCOM level				
	Logic connecting the program to goals (logic model)			
	Program design and budget assumptions			
	Relative opportunity costs			
	Alternative programs			
	Diminishing marginal utility			
		Process followed?		
		Full inputs?		
		Quotas filled?		
		Rules obeyed?		
		Steps?		
		Accuracy?		
		Timeliness?		
		Use of funds?		
		Full outputs?		
			Measurable improvements in relationships, capabilities, and access	
			More specific objectives at country/COCOM level	
				Bang for the buck

programs. Recalling the authorities associated with the programs summarized in Chapter Two and the Air Force's budgetary controls—less than 1 percent of the O&M account; less than 1 percent of the R&D account—top-level decisions about the needs for a program and its design and theory are reserved to the highest levels of leadership within DoD, typically within OSD, although perhaps not exclusively. At least in theory, Air Force stakeholders would concentrate on matters of process and implementation, outcomes and effects, and cost-effectiveness.

However, many stakeholders consulted for this study stated that their actual stakes extend beyond their formal authorities. Many believe that they exercise both formal influence and decisionmaking given their responsibilities as sanctioned in the authorities, but that they also exercise informal authority, which most often takes the form of advocacy. That is, they believe that their jobs involve advocating decisions and policy options in their interactions with the higher echelons of the chain of command. Therefore, they may want to have assessments at their disposal that may actually exceed the scope of the decisions that they are authorized to make. Allowing assessments that go beyond a particular stakeholder's authority can create some complexities to the degree that it violates the authorities-decisions-assessment relationship. Assuming that the Air Force finds value in stakeholders who advocate decisions or positions beyond the scope of their formal authorities, the Air Force can accommodate this complexity by assessing all Air Force security cooperation programs across the entire hierarchy of evaluation.

Implementing Security Cooperation Assessments

Legal authorities, set forth in U.S.C. Title 10 and Title 22, establish the principal departmental divisions of labor, but Title 10, especially, gives DoD considerable leeway on how to manage the programs within its domain. Strategy and planning documents, such as the GEF, describe the ends, ways, and means of security cooperation for DoD. However, they do not say much about program execution, including assessment.[2] Many security cooperation programs have accompanying directives or operating instructions that specify the program's objectives, how resources are allotted and expended, and the various stakeholder responsibilities. A review of those directives and instructions, depending on how detailed they are, can, in most cases, make assigning assessment roles fairly straightforward. However, not all programs have associated directives or operating instructions. Many, such as the WIF, are governed only by broad U.S.C. Title 10 guidance, specifically, U.S.C. Title 10, §1051 and §168.[3] In the absence of more specific directives or instructions, the use of broad selection criteria can be helpful in thinking through the appropriate assessment roles of each stakeholder.

The Air Force plays roles in three general categories of security cooperation programs. The first category represents those Title 10 programs that the Air Force manages—such programs as LATAM Coop and MPEP, among others. The second category contains Title 10 programs managed by organizations other than the Air Force. DoD-controlled programs offer useful examples of this category, including the Logistics Support for Allied Forces Participating in Combined Operations (Global Lift and Sustain). The Air Force is clearly involved—it supplies the lift—but OSD makes the decisions, specifically, the determination that "the support is essential to the success of the combined operation and without it, the foreign military forces would be unable to participate in the combined operation," with the concurrence of the Secretary of State.[4]

The third category of programs is found under Title 22 in the realm of security assistance, where the Air Force administers and executes specific activities while seeking to provide oversight and influence policy, but where the primary stakeholders are in the DSCA, OSD,

---

[2] For example, the GEF states that the services must provide output-oriented assessments of the programs they conduct in support of the COCOMs. But the GEF does not provide details on how these programs should be assessed over time.

[3] U.S. Department of Defense, Office of the Inspector General, *Joint Warfighting and Readiness, DoD Execution of the Warsaw Initiative Program*, D-2005-085, Washington, D.C., July 1, 2005.

[4] U.S.C. Title 10, §127c, Public Law (PL) 109-364 S1201 of National Defense Authorization Act for FY 2007 (new authority) and PL 109-148 S9009.

and DOS.[5] FMS cases, including the Canadian C-17 support case examined in Chapter Four, are examples of this category.

Title 10 Security Cooperation Programs Managed by the Air Force

For programs entirely under the Air Force's authority, assessments across the entire hierarchy of evaluation are possible. The key is to remember that the Air Force should assess only where it has decisions to make about the program. In other words, the rationale for assessing security cooperation programs is to provide information that will support decisionmaking:

- Does the program advance objectives of importance to the Air Force?
- Is the program's design and theory consistent with the expectations for security cooperation programs generally as described in Chapter Two?
- Is the program operated in a way that is consistent with its authorizing and managing directives, regulations, and instructions?
- Are the program's outcomes and effects consistent with our expectations?
- Is the program cost-effective?

Title 10 Security Cooperation Programs Not Managed by the Air Force

Within this class of programs, the Air Force faces no decisions with regard to the need for the program or the quality of its design and theory, but other stakeholders do, typically in OSD and the COCOMs. Others—the primary principal stakeholders for these programs—will probably have responsibilities for the cost-effectiveness of the programs and thus the cost-effectiveness assessments. Air Force involvement is likely to center on assessment of the process and implementation (e.g., are we following instructions?) and on outcome (e.g., what percentage of participants graduated from a course?).

---

[5]   U.S.C. Title 22, §2761, §2762, §2769, §2763; AECA U.S.C. §21–22, §29 (Arms Export Control Act).

Title 22 Security Assistance Programs

This category of programs also can be subject to the full scope of assessments, even though not all decisions are within the Air Force's authority. DCS and FMS require approval of DoD and DOS and, in some cases, Congress. However, Air Force commands, such as AFMC and AETC, are involved in case development and execution. Air Force components may be involved with on-site training, as in the Polish F-16 and the Singapore F-15 cases. Furthermore, DCS programs require a license that must have the approval of the Air Force before the sale and export of munitions or sensitive equipment can be completed. Therefore, those stakeholders should also conduct assessments to support and improve those decisions.

Assessment Functions

In general, the Air Force, other DoD, and DOS organizations can and do perform four functional assessment roles with respect to security cooperation programs. In some cases, these functions are clearly spelled out in government policy directives and program instructions. In other cases, they must be inferred by taking into account the character of the organization and the extent of its *de jure* and *de facto* decisionmaking authority. The following are proposed definitions for the four stakeholder assessment functions:

- **Data collector.** Responsible for collecting and aggregating data for a particular kind of programmatic assessment from internal and external sources according to standards set by the assessor organization
- **Assessor.** Responsible for setting data collection standards for a particular kind of programmatic assessment and for evaluating programs using methods suitable for the types of assessment being performed
- **Reviewer.** Responsible for helping assessors develop data collection standards and evaluation methods appropriate for the kind of assessment for which they are responsible, as well as for conducting periodic inspections or audits to ensure that program assessments are being properly executed

- **Integrator.** Responsible for organizing and synthesizing programmatic assessments to meet OSD and Air Force requirements for the GEF, the AFGPS, the Capabilities Portfolio Management System, and the PPBE process.

These assessment roles are intended to help guide assessment behavior, not to restrict the range of assessment assignments that a particular organization is allowed to undertake. As the next section argues, the Air Force and other organizations may fill a variety of security cooperation assessment roles, depending on the category of program and level of assessment under discussion.

Air Force Assessment Organizations

As discussed in previous chapters, Air Force organizations already assess certain aspects of security cooperation programs. Inspections at the unit level that assess compliance are the most common; they are really assessments of compliance and implementation. Did the unit follow the regulations? Keep the appropriate records? Meet the standards? Other entities, including Program Assessment and Evaluation-like offices (perhaps HQ AF/A8), the AFAA, and A9 offices throughout the Air Force, conduct assessments that fall into the domain of need for the program, design and theory, outcomes and effects, and cost-effectiveness, respectively. The Air Force, therefore, may have the right organizations to perform many security cooperation-related assessments and could task these organizations to perform these assessments if the Air Force is committed to the spirit and intent of assessments as articulated in the GEF.

Deciding which organization is the appropriate one to carry out assessments will depend in part on the category the program in question occupies—is it a Title 10 program within the Air Force's authority, a non–Air Force Title 10 program, or perhaps a Title 22 security assistance program?

However, published authorities and responsibilities cannot serve as the sole basis for assigning assessment roles. The existing documentation rarely spells out these roles in detail, and in many cases, more than one organization can make a plausible claim for a particular assessment assignment. Legal authorities, set forth in Title 10 and Title 22, establish the principal departmental divisions of labor, but Title 10, in particular, gives DoD considerable leeway in how it manages programs within its domain. Strategy and planning documents, such as the GEF and the AFGPS, describe the ends, ways, and means of security cooperation for DoD and the Air Force. However, they do not say much about program execution, including assessment.[6] AFPD 16-1 gives SAF/IA the responsibility for integrating and overseeing Air Force international programs and policies without indicating how this responsibility should be exercised or reconciled with the responsibilities of other organizations. Security cooperation program instructions, when they exist, do establish specific managerial responsibilities, but they are generally silent on how programs should be evaluated.

Thus, in many cases, assigning specific assessment responsibilities to particular organizations will require looking beyond relevant laws, policies, and regulations. In particular, it is important that Air Force officials pay close attention to an organization's *capabilities*—in particular its resources, expertise, proximity, and opportunity—as well as to its *objectivity*—i.e., the extent of its interest in specific assessment results.

Proposed Organizational Assignments and Criteria for Selecting Stakeholder Roles

Many DoD organizations might serve as data collectors, assessors, reviewers, and integrators for Air Force–managed security cooperation programs and the five levels of assessment decisions. A key goal is to inject a greater level of objectivity into the overall assessment processes, thus moving away from the current, largely self-assessment approach to BPC programs. These ends, especially in the absence of directives and

---

[6]   For example, the GEF says that the services must provide output-oriented assessments of the programs they conduct in support of the COCOMs, and within the Air Force, this responsibility has been given to SAF/IA.

instructions, should inform the process of assigning various stakeholders with assessment roles. Some examples include the following:

- delineate assessment responsibilities across several stakeholders to account for different levels of organizational authority and expertise and to inject as much objectivity into the process as possible
- identify a single organization with a close connection to the program at hand to be ultimately responsible for gathering and collating assessment data, although data collection will often involve a number of individuals and organizations from different parts of DoD (and even from outside)
- recognize that in some cases, the data collector and the assessor will be the same individual; more likely, these positions will be held by persons within the same organization
- ensure that the assessor and the reviewer are not the same person, although they may be within the same organization (even this is not ideal)
- ensure that reviewers, especially, and integrators pay careful attention to which data are collected and which attributes are selected as outputs and outcomes lest attributes be designed to fit what the program has done, not necessarily the goals for it
- maintain strong linkages between integrators and program stakeholders to develop both as much standardization as possible and as much clarity on best practices in security cooperation assessment. In addition, integrators should develop mechanisms for storing assessment information (so that it is available to as wide a group of program stakeholders as possible) and synthesizing this information for various decisionmaking purposes.

Assessment Roles for Air Force–Managed Programs

Tables 5.2, 5.3, and 5.4 suggest organizations that might serve as data collectors, assessors, reviewers, and integrators for the three basic categories of Air Force security cooperation programs and the five levels of assessment decisions. Table 5.2 focuses on suggested organizational assignments for Air Force–managed programs. The table attempts to keep faith with the dictum from Chapter Three, "only assess when there's a decision to be made," but within the context of the Air Force. As a military service, the Air Force relies on staff practices to collect, analyze, assess, and recommend a course of action—a decision—which is then presented to senior leaders for action. Therefore, we have formulated a series of assessment roles that comport with military staff practices.

Tables 5.2, 5.3, and 5.4 are provided for illustrative purposes to show how, using the above logic, assessment roles may be assigned to program stakeholders. These assignments are generic and may not fit the needs or requirements of some programs. They should be further reviewed by the DoD security cooperation community before they are proposed for approval. These proposed organizational assignments are only a first step in establishing an integrated structure of assessment roles and responsibilities that could eventually encompass service- and COCOM-managed security cooperation programs, as well as security assistance programs overseen by DOS.

Table 5.2
Potential Assessment Roles for Air Force–Managed Programs

Assessment Decision	Potential Data Collector	Potential Assessor	Potential Reviewer	Potential Integrator
Need for the program	Program manager or SAF/IA	AFCS	AFCS	SAF/IA
Design and theory	Program manager	Program manager and AF/A9	IG and/or AFAA	SAF/IA
Process and implementation	Program manager	Program manager and AF/A9	IG and/or AFAA	SAF/IA
Outcomes and effects	Program manager	SAF/IA	SAF/IA	SAF/IA
Cost-effectiveness	Program manager	AFCS	AFCS	SAF/IA

As noted above, the Air Force should be involved in the full range of assessment decisions—from program need to cost-effectiveness—when it comes to Title 10 programs, such as MPEP and LATAM Coop, over which DoD has delegated full managerial authority to the services.

Data Collector. In our view, data collection is largely a matter of capability. The program managers generally have the most capability and most complete knowledge of program details; hence, they are best positioned to gather and collate information, from a variety of stakeholders inside and outside the Air Force, on the need for an existing Air Force program. However, SAF/IA is probably in the best position to gather data on the need for a program that has not yet been established. Once a program has been established, program managers may remain the best suited to collect assessment-related data from internal and external sources that would support assessments of the suitability of the program's design and theory, its operational practices and implementation, the outcomes and effects of the program, and its cost-effectiveness.

Assessor. Determining which organizations will be assessors should be based on a combination of authority, capability, and objectivity. Authority can be over a decisionmaking process, such as that exercised by a program manager, and, possibly, by AF/A9 to a certain extent. Capability can derive from resident expertise in determining requirements and assessment criteria or from day-to-day exposure to the consequences of the design, output, and outcome of Air Force security cooperation programs in partner countries (in the case of SAF/IA). AFCS's objectivity as an assessor stems from the balancing role that it plays in advising senior Air Force leaders on a portfolio of operational and nonoperational programs. Moreover, AFCS enjoys an Air Force–wide perspective that makes its deliberations more objective, and it also retains wide authority for leading and shaping Air Force capabilities including, and also beyond, security cooperation.

Reviewer. The reviewer role is best handled for the most part by specialized agencies with the proper authority, capability, and objectivity. An exception may be AFCS's invaluable perspective, seasoned judgment, and skills at managing diverse priorities when it comes to evaluating the need for a program. Another possible exception arises if there is the need to review whether the outcome objectives were met, which should probably be handled by SAF/IA, since SAF/IA sets the outcomes in its Global Partnership Strategy. In addition to financial audits, AFAA is empowered to conduct performance audits that "provide assurance or conclusions based on an evaluation of sufficient, appropriate evidence against stated criteria. . . ."[7] Performance audit objectives differ widely but can include assessments of program effectiveness, economy, and efficiency; internal control; and compliance. Such objectives would seem to meet the requirements for reviews of security cooperation program design, execution, and outcome. Alternatively, the IG can provide an independent and objective management review of such Air Force–wide processes as security cooperation, if requested by senior leaders. The IG also conducts compliance and field inspections to independently assess "Air Force operational readiness, efficiency, discipline, economy, and effectiveness" in cooperation with MAJCOM IG teams.[8]

Integrator. It makes policy sense for SAF/IA to serve as the principal integrator of Air Force security cooperation assessments, as it is the "focal point . . . for matters involving U.S. Air Force international interests."[9] This role seems especially appropriate given OSD's requirement, as enunciated in the GEF, that the services assess the outputs of the security cooperation programs they are funding in support of the COCOMs. Presumably, the OSD Partnership Strategy, the manager of the Building Partnerships Portfolio within DoD's Capabilities Portfolio Management System, would be responsible for integrating service assessments with outcome-oriented assessments developed by the COCOMs. In addition, as an assessment integrator, SAF/IA would have a better opportunity to raise the profile of security cooperation programs within the Air Force PPBE process through its representation in the AFCS. This profile could be increased to an even greater extent if the Air Force were to create an AFCS expert panel, chaired by SAF/IA,

---

[7] U.S. Government Accountability Office, *Government Auditing Standards, Revision*, GAO-07-731G, Washington, D.C., July 27, 2007.

[8] U.S. Air Force, *Inspector General Activities*, AFI 90-201, November 22, 2004b, pp. 38–42.

[9] U.S. Air Force, 1993.

akin to the existing mission and mission-support centers of expertise, which would be solely devoted to security cooperation.

Assessment Roles for Other DoD-Managed Programs

As Table 5.3 indicates, the Air Force should have a limited role in assessing DoD security cooperation programs—for example, the five DoD regional centers or such CJCS Exercises as FLEXIBLE RESPONSE—for which OSD, the Joint Staff, and the COCOMs have the managerial lead.

The Air Force's assessment roles for programs managed by other DoD agencies largely stem from its regional components' subordinate relationship to the COCOMs. For example, with respect to traditional commander-in-chief activities, in which the Air Force participates as an implementing agency, the components may be best positioned to assess program design, execution, and outcome, as well as to provide information to the COCOM on the potential need for particular Air Force–related activities. However, official assessments of program need and costs/benefits should probably be done at the COCOM or OSD level so that factors unrelated to air and space power can be considered.

Although Air Force components may have some responsibility for providing assessment-related data, the primary data collector is likely

Table 5.3
Assessment Roles for Other DoD-Managed Programs

Assessment Decision	Data Collector	Assessor	Reviewer	Integrator
Need for the program	Program manager or OSD/COCOM	OSD COCOM	OSD COCOM	OSD COCOM
Design and theory	Program manager	COCOM components	OSD COCOM	OSD COCOM
Process and implementation	Program manager	COCOM components	OSD COCOM	OSD COCOM
Outcomes and effects	Program manager	COCOM components	OSD COCOM	OSD COCOM
Cost-effectiveness	Program manager	OSD COCOM	OSD COCOM	OSD COCOM

to be the program manager, which in most instances will be under the authority of the COCOM or OSD. (The COCOM or OSD will necessarily have to take direct responsibility for collecting data on the need for a program that is under consideration but does not currently exist.) Similarly, the responsibility for the review and integration aspects of assessment should probably be given to the COCOMs and OSD, particularly for DoD programs that are not managed by the Air Force.[10]

Assessment Roles for Security Assistance Programs

In contrast to some Title 10 programs, the authorities and responsibilities for most forms of Title 22 security assistance are clearly defined in laws, policies, and regulations. Thus, it is a relatively straightforward procedure to propose functional assessment roles for particular organizations in the Air Force, other parts of DoD, and DOS (see Table 5.4).

The primary data collection role for most security assistance programs is probably best performed by SAOs in U.S. embassies overseas (when assessing the need for a new program) and by CONUS-based security assistance case managers and training organizations (in the case of ongoing program needs assessments as well as design, execution, outcome, and cost-benefit assessments). SAOs, also called Office of Defense Cooperation, Military Groups, and Joint U.S. Military Advisory and Assistance Groups, are designed to elicit information on the security assistance requirements of partner countries. Once an Air Force–related security assistance connection has been established through FMS, FMF, IMET, or another funding mechanism, training and equipping managers within AFSAC and AFSAT should collect information on the progress of particular cases from Air Force product centers, training facilities, and schools, as well as SAOs, COCOMs, components, and partner countries.

---

[10] In fact, the OSD Partnership Strategy is considering creating a new office that would undertake these assessment responsibilities for OSD-managed programs, including the regional centers, the WIF, the Combating Terrorism Fellowship Program (CTFP), the State Partnership Program, the Overseas Humanitarian Disaster and Civic Assistance Program, and the Section 1206 Global Train and Equip Program. RAND is assisting OSD/Policy in this effort.

Table 5.4
Assessment Roles for Security Assistance Programs

Assessment Decision	Data Collector	Assessor	Reviewer	Integrator
Need for the program	Case manager Training organization, or SAO	SAF/IA OSD	DOS	DSCA
Design and theory	Case manager Training organization	AFMC AETC	SAF/IA	DSCA
Process and implementation	Case manager Training organization	AFMC AETC	SAF/IA	DSCA
Outcomes and effects	Case manager Training organization	Components	COCOM	DSCA
Cost-effectiveness	Case manager Training organization	SAF/IA OSD	DOS	DSCA

Given the complicated security assistance authority structure, the assessor and reviewer functions must be divided among several DOS and DoD organizations. As key policy and resourcing bodies, SAF/IA and OSD/Policy could jointly assess the need for and the costs and benefits of Air Force security assistance programs. Functional service MAJCOMs, such as AFMC and AETC, which oversee U.S. and partner country acquisition, training, and education, are in the best position to evaluate security assistance program design and execution. Because of their overseas orientation, regional components, including USAFE and Pacific Air Forces (PACAF), are well-suited to assess long-term program outcomes, such as demonstrable changes in partner air force capability.

Potential security assistance program reviewers—with the requisite authority, capability, and objectivity—include DOS's Resource Management Bureau (for needs and cost-benefit assessments), SAF/IA and its counterpart offices in the Army and Navy (for design and execution assessments), and the geographic COCOMs (for outcome assessments).

With its new security assistance information management system and responsibility for the day-to-day management of DoD security assistance, the DSCA is the logical candidate to integrate various security assistance assessments for decisionmakers in both the Executive Branch and Congress.

Training for Assessments

The study team has identified one issue that needs to be addressed before implementing a new Air Force security cooperation assessment framework: the availability of personnel with the required skills to carry out this task. Most Air Force stakeholders have expressed some concern over whether their organizations have the necessary skill sets that will allow them to contribute comprehensively to the assessment process. Some basic training may help to address any deficiency, bridging the gap between capabilities and expectations.

Discussions with AETC have indicated that Air Force operations research analysts are declining in numbers. The only fields to grow, but only slightly, are war-gaming, weapon systems testing, and simulation. Given this limitation, it may be worthwhile for the Air Force to work with other key internal and external stakeholders, such as AETC, DSCA, and the Defense Institute for Security Assistance Management, to develop a new course on security cooperation assessments. The goal of this course would be to better prepare data collectors, assessors, reviewers, and integrators for their respective assessment responsibilities. Such courses could target civilian Air Force international affairs professionals and regional/policy affairs specialist officers. A basic course focus could include assessment design, data collection, evaluation, and integration methods. Subsequently, advanced coursework could include techniques for aggregating and interpreting assessment results to support security cooperation decisionmaking and analytical skills to support comparison and valuation of security cooperation programs.

A Proposed Air Force Assessment Approach

To summarize the assessment approach described in this monograph, we propose that the Air Force take four basic steps.

First, members of the Air Force security cooperation community need to reach a consensus regarding the definitions of, and linkages among, the key elements of the program assessment framework. In particular, they should

- define what constitutes a program for assessment purposes
- identify key stakeholders for each Air Force program
- associate programs with security cooperation ends, focus areas, and ways
- separate programs into authorities and management bins.

Second, the Air Force needs to determine the assessment roles and responsibilities for each program stakeholder, by level of assessment.

Third, program stakeholders need to develop appropriate assessment questions for each level of assessment and security cooperation way.

Finally, the Air Force should implement a comprehensive security cooperation assessment framework, perhaps starting with the Title 10 programs it directly manages. Figure 5.1 illustrates one way this might be accomplished.

Using the assessment questions developed in step three, the Air Force would task appropriate subordinate elements—the data collectors identified in Table 5.3—to collect and provide the necessary data to the assessing organizations—the organizations listed in the "assessor" column of Table 5.3. These organizations would perform the actual assessments. Periodically, specialized reviewing organizations, also identified in Table 5.3, would check the methods and results of the assessors.

Once the assessments are completed and reviewed, they could be passed to the assessment integrator, probably SAF/IA, given the office's responsibilities for security cooperation. SAF/IA would organize the assessments and recommendations and present them in a way that

Figure 5.1
Implementing an Air Force Assessment Framework

Air Force security cooperation ways

Education	Experimentation	Personnel exchanges	International arms cooperation
Equipment	Training	Facilities and infrastructure	Humanitarian assistance
Exercises	Defense and military contacts	Information and Intelligence cooperation	Workshops, conferences and seminars
		International agreements	

Security cooperation programs are the units of measure

Levels of assessment

Assessment of cost-effectiveness

Assessment of outcomes and impacts

Assessment of process and implementation

Assessment of design and theory

Assessment of need for the program

Reviewers inspect or audit program assessments

Data collectors provide relevant info for security cooperation assessments

Integrators organize and synthesize program assessments

Assessors evaluate programs, ideally across all five assessment levels, for effectiveness relative to select security cooperation focus areas

Decisionmakers use assessments to determine security cooperation resources, policy, and strategy

RAND *MG868-5.1*

would make it easy for senior leaders to review before making decisions on each program assessed. The entire process might be synchronized to support the annual budget cycle. As a result of this assessment procedure, Air Force senior leaders would have at their disposal a wealth of information on Air Force security cooperation programs, which would allow them to satisfy the assessment requirement in the GEF. This information would also equip leaders to be better prepared to make trade-offs among security cooperation programs when resources are constrained.

Conclusions

This chapter has suggested an approach that would allow the Air Force to implement the security cooperation assessment framework proposed in this monograph. The framework includes ways to overcome the impediments to sound assessments of security cooperation programs by organizing Air Force organizations to conduct the assessments. It also suggests appropriate supported and supporting stakeholder roles.

Bringing this approach to fruition would require that the Air Force complete a number of important tasks for key Air Force security cooperation stakeholders, to include

- assigning supported and supporting roles
- delegating authority to develop assessment questions and data collection formats
- tasking specific organizations for data collection and support
- tasking specific organizations to conduct the assessments and specifying the levels on the hierarchy of evaluation to be addressed
- establishing time lines and frequencies for assessments, recognizing that it will be necessary to collect time-series data for several years to conduct program-level assessments.

Despite the many obstacles that must be overcome to accurately measure the direct contributions of security cooperation programs to the end states articulated by OSD and the COCOMs, the analysis presented here suggests that it is possible to conduct many security cooperation assessments that are consistent with the spirit and intent of the GEF and the AFGPS. The final chapter provides specific recommendations that will enable the Air Force to move forward with a new security cooperation assessment framework.

CHAPTER SIX

Conclusions and Recommendations

Conclusions

This monograph argues that an enhanced assessment framework is needed to enable the Air Force to make informed resource and policy decisions about its security cooperation programs. Moreover, it is imperative that stakeholder roles and missions, as defined in the authorities, be clearly articulated to determine their appropriate assessment responsibilities.

First, the study team recommends that the Air Force incorporate a program-level assessment into its current security cooperation assessment process to meet OSD and Air Force requirements. Program assessments will help the Air Force to form a more complete picture, enabling it to answer questions from internal and external stakeholders regarding the relevance, design, efficiency, effect, and cost-effectiveness of its security cooperation efforts with partner air forces.

Second, it is important that Air Force stakeholders conduct security cooperation assessments with the intent to inform decisionmaking. As a first step, the Air Force should focus its assessment efforts on the security cooperation programs it manages. Information gathered should be provided to OSD and to appropriate Air Force stakeholders. With this information, the Air Force should seek to influence the OSD-led Building Partnerships Portfolio management and the Air Force PPBE processes.

Third, because of limited assessment guidance and the need for efficient assessment processes, the Air Force should clarify and specify the roles and responsibilities of stakeholders in making security cooperation assessments. Again, the Air Force should focus first on the programs that it directly manages. It then should work with OSD, DSCA, the COCOMs, and other major external stakeholders to spell out the assessment roles and responsibilities of Air Force organizations involved in the implementation of security cooperation programs not managed by the Air Force. In general, the MAJCOMs should be responsible for aggregating lower-level Air Force assessments (i.e., needs, design and theory, and process). Higher-level assessments (i.e., outcomes and costs and benefits) would come in part from Air Staff, OSD/Policy, DSCA, the COCOMs, and DOS.

The following recommendations for implementing the assessment framework are specified in relation to the following four topics: guidance, assessment management, assessment activities, and training.

Recommendations

Guidance

The Air Force should continue to work closely with OSD to clarify program assessment responsibilities in the GEF. Questions that need to be clarified include the following:

- Which programs should the Air Force assess and in what priority?[1]
- What kind of assessments should be provided, e.g., output, outcome, costs and benefits?
- What are the enduring goals that need to be addressed over time?

Consider including an annex on assessments in the AFGPS. Such an annex should

- explain that the overall need for programmatic analysis is to provide input into the OSD-led Building Partnerships Portfolio management process and perhaps the campaign support plans process

---

[1] Programs that the Air Force directly manages should be the highest priority.

- translate GEF end states into achievable and measurable Air Force program objectives
- task Air Force stakeholders (i.e., the designated program assessor organizations) to develop assessment questions relative to their programs and provide those questions to SAF/IA
- encourage stakeholders to share those questions with other relevant program managers, possibly in preparation for the annual SAF/IA global partnerships conference (see the discussion below).

Consider assigning the responsibilities for data collection, assessment, assessment review, and assessment integration to stakeholders. Distinguish the roles and responsibilities among Title 10 programs that the Air Force manages, Title 10 programs in which the Air Force participates, and Title 22 security assistance programs that the Air Force primarily executes.

Consider updating key Air Force security cooperation doctrine and strategy/guidance documents to emphasize stakeholder roles and responsibilities as well as the importance of conducting assessments. Specifically, AFM 16-101 and AFPD 16-1 should be updated to specify assessment roles and responsibilities for all Air Force security cooperation stakeholders. Moreover, the Air Force should emphasize the importance of security cooperation assessments in the Air Force campaign support plan, APPG, and other guidance documents.

Assessment Management

Attempt to leverage assessment capacity and processes within the Air Force where they already exist. The Air Force should thoroughly review the assessment capabilities for Air Force security cooperation, for example, within the Air Staff (e.g., AF/A9, AF/A8), the AFAA, and the inspectors general at key Air Force commands and organizations. SAF/IA should engage the relevant potential assessment organizations to build relationships and formally expand security cooperation assessment responsibilities, where possible.

Emphasize security cooperation assessments as a focus area for the next annual SAF/IA global partnerships conference. Participants should come prepared to discuss inputs, outputs, outcomes, and the costs and benefits of their respective programs and activities, in addition to general successes and challenges that they may be experiencing. All managers and assessors of programs where the Air Force has primary management responsibilities should be invited to attend the event, and at least one representative from each program should attend the assessment breakout session of the conference. Consider having an independent organization with security cooperation assessment experience run the assessment breakout session to ensure a quality output and objectivity.

Ensure that SAF/IA is the assessment integrator for programs involving the Air Force, rather than collecting data on specific programs and activities. The results of the assessment process should be integrated by SAF/IA and then provided to key decisionmakers (e.g., SAF, the CSAF, OSD/PA&E, and OSD/Policy). Consider ways to ensure that stakeholders are adequately resourced, particularly with manpower, skills, training, and funding, to perform the assessment roles assigned to them. As a first step, SAF/IA should consider holding a two-star-level meeting to recommend assessment roles and responsibilities among Air Force stakeholders.

Consider creating an AFCS panel, chaired by SAF/IA, devoted to the security cooperation mission. This panel would enable HQ AF/A8 to better assess the relative costs and benefits of operational and security cooperation programs for decisions related to the PPBE process. Within this process, the Air Force should identify *all* programs and activities it manages that support building partnerships.

Assessment Activities

Consider a time-phased approach to data collection in which standardized assessment questions are answered to compare and contrast the results. Comprehensive assessments will be possible only if questions and metrics are standardized and tracked over time. Encourage Air Force stakeholders, especially those involved in the planning and implementation of Air Force–managed programs, to develop a standardized list of assessment questions, along the lines of those articulated in Chapter Two of this monograph.

Ensure that stakeholder objectivity is maintained in the program assessment framework. Specifically, we recommend the following five-step process:

- Data (e.g., after-action reports and administrative data) should be aggregated by program managers.
- Data should then be passed to program assessors.
- Data should then be passed to program reviewers who are not directly or personally invested directly in the program being reviewed.
- Finally, data should be passed to assessment integrators, who, again, are not directly or personally invested in the program being reviewed.
- After the reports are integrated, they should be provided to relevant internal and external decisionmakers.

Knowledgebase should be the repository for programmatic assessments. Programmatic assessments should be collected and disseminated on Knowledgebase, whenever possible. In addition, SAF/IA should continue to explore options to use Knowledgebase for program and other assessment purposes and, possibly, for assessment training purposes, as discussed below.

Training

SAF/IA should consider working with the AFIT's Center for Operational Analysis, Air University, AETC, and DSCA to develop a professional curriculum for security cooperation assessments. Such courses should aim to prepare data collectors, assessors, reviewers, and integrators for their respective assessment responsibilities. Courses could target civilian international affairs professionals and regional/policy affairs specialist officers within the Air Force and teach assessment design, data collection, evaluation, and integration methods. Advanced coursework could include techniques for aggregating and interpreting assessment results to support security cooperation decisionmaking and analytical skills to support comparison and valuation of security cooperation programs. Courses could be online or in the classroom, or a combination of both.

Air Force Security Cooperation Programs (Illustrative)

Table A.1
Air Force Security Cooperation Programs

Program	Authority	Explanation of Program and Objectives
Category 1: Title 10 Programs Managed by the Air Force		
Air and Trade Show Participation	U.S.C. Title 10, §2539 Department of Defense Instruction (DoDI) 7230.8 AFI 16-110 PL 102-484 §1082	Participation in international air shows and trade exhibitions allows the United States to showcase its defense technology and weapon systems, thereby facilitating opportunities for cooperative research, development, and acquisition
Aviation Leadership Program	U.S.C. Title 10, §§9381–9383 Department of Defense Directive (DoDD) 2010.12 Federal Aviation Authority, §544c	This program authorizes the participation of foreign and U.S. military defense personnel in post-undergraduate flying training and tactical leadership programs in Southwest Asia without charge to participating foreign countries
Bilateral and multilateral forums	U.S.C. Title 10 AFI 16-110	These forums allow senior defense officials to participate in organizations that facilitate cooperation between the United States and its allies in military research, development, and acquisition
Bilateral regional cooperation programs	U.S.C. Title 10, §1051	These programs enable defense personnel from developing countries to attend bilateral or regional conferences, seminars, or similar meetings that are in the national security interests of the United States

Table A.1—Continued

Program	Authority	Explanation of Program and Objectives
Cooperative Research, Development, Testing, Evaluation, and Production (CRDTE&P)	U.S.C. Title 10, §§2350a, 2358 PL 101-189 AFI 16-110 ("Nunn Amendment")	CRDTE&P allows for cooperative R&D projects on defense equipment and munitions with NATO and other friendly countries. The program's aim is to improve common capabilities through the application of emerging technology
Defense Personnel Exchange Program	U.S.C. Title 10, B11168 PL 104-201 §108	This program provides for a reciprocal exchange of military or civilian defense personnel with allied or friendly countries, to familiarize participants with the operations of the other party and foster mutual understanding and cooperation between governments
Defense RDT&E, Information Exchange Program (IEP)	U.S.C. Title 10 DoDI 2015.4 AFI 16-110	This program allows for the reciprocal exchange of scientific and technical information with allied and friendly nations, to explore future technology cooperation and multinational force compatibility
Engineering and Scientist Exchange Program	U.S.C. Title 10, 168 note PL 104-201	This program provides for the exchange of civilian and military engineers and scientists between the United States and foreign countries to RDT&E facilities to increase cooperation and technical exchange in the R&D environment
Foreign Comparative Test Program	U.S.C. Title 10, §2360a(g) AFI 16-110	This program authorizes the evaluation of defense equipment, munitions, and technologies developed by U.S. allies and other friendly countries to determine their ability to satisfy U.S. military requirements
LATAM Coop	U.S.C. Title 10, §1050	The program provides funds for visits, exchanges, and seminars to advance cooperation between the United States and Latin American countries
Military academy student exchanges (U.S. Air Force Academy)	U.S.C. Title 10, §9345	The program allows for the exchange of cadets between the U.S. Air Force Academy and foreign air force institutions

Table A.1—Continued

Program	Authority	Explanation of Program and Objectives
Military-to-military contacts	U.S.C. Title 10, §§168, 1051, 2010	Military-to-military contacts and comparable activities are designed to encourage the democratic orientation of defense establishments and military forces of other countries
MPEP	DoDD 5230.20 AFI 16-107	The MPEP is a one-year exchange of military personnel in equivalent grades and specialties with foreign nations to enhance the ability of the U.S. military to perform coalition operations by building and expanding international relationships
NATO forums	U.S.C. Title 10 AFI 16-110 DoDI 2010.4	NATO forums advise the North Atlantic Council on the development and procurement of equipment for NATO forces; they promote standardization and cooperative research and information exchanges within the alliance
Ops-to-ops talks	U.S.C. Title 10 CSAF Memo (2000)	These talks are designed to enhance ops-to-ops relationships between the U.S. Air Force and a select group of allies and partner air forces
Professional military education student exchange	FAA §544a	The exchange provides for no-cost, reciprocal professional military student exchanges
UNIFIED ENGAGEMENT regional BPC seminars	U.S.C. Title 10	The seminars are designed to enhance bilateral and multilateral relationships between the U.S. Air Force and select allies and partner air forces
U.S. Air Force Exercise Program	U.S.C. Title 10	This program includes bilateral and multilateral exercises, such as Red Flag, designed to enhance interoperability between the U.S. Air Force and select allies and partner air forces
Category 2: Title 10 Programs Not Managed by the Air Force		
Acquisition and cross-servicing agreements	U.S.C. Title 10, §§2341–2350 PL 109-364 §1202	These agreements allow the U.S. military to provide logistics support, supplies, and services on a reciprocal basis to foreign military forces and to lend defense articles to countries participating in coalition operations in Iraq or Afghanistan

Table A.1—Continued

Program	Authority	Explanation of Program and Objectives
Afghan security forces training	Title IX, PL 109-289 Title I, PL 110-128	The program allows DoD to provide equipment, supplies, services, and training to the Afghan security forces, to enable the Afghan government to increase its counterinsurgency capabilities and assume greater responsibility for security
ANG State Partnership Program	Title 32 National Defense Authorization Act, 1993 (annual)	The program links U.S. states with partner countries for the purpose of supporting U.S. national security goals; objectives include the promotion of military subordination to civilian authority, development of democratic institutions, and fostering open market economies
Andean Counterdrug Initiative (Plan Colombia)	PL 106-246	The plan provides training and support to national police and military forces by providing communications and intelligence systems and maintenance and operations of host country aerial eradication aircraft related to counternarcotics activities
Build the Capacity of the Pakistan Frontier Corps Program	PL 110-181 §1206	The program provides equipment, supplies, and training to enhance the Pakistanis' ability to conduct counterterrorism operations along the border between Pakistan and Afghanistan
CJCS Exercise Program	U.S.C. Title 10, §§166a, 193 DoDD 5100.1	The exercises provide combatant commanders with their primary means to train battle staffs and forces in joint and combined operations and often include foreign militaries and coalition partners
Commanders Emergency Response Program	PL 110-181 §1205	This program provides funds for military commanders in Iraq and Afghanistan to respond to urgent humanitarian relief and reconstruction requirement
CRDTE&P	U.S.C. Title 10, §§2350a, 2358 PL 101-189 AFI 16-110 ("Nunn Amendment")	CRDTE&P allows for cooperative R&D projects on defense equipment and munitions with NATO and other friendly countries to improve common capabilities through the application of emerging technology

Table A.1—Continued

Program	Authority	Explanation of Program and Objectives
Cooperative Threat Reduction Program (Nunn-Lugar Program)	PL 104-201 §1501 PL 109-289	The program helps former countries of the Soviet Union destroy chemical, nuclear, and other weapons and establish verifiable safeguards against proliferation to reduce the threat of WMD proliferation
DoD Counterdrug Program	PL 101-510, §§1004, 1033	OSD may provide nonreimbursed assistance and training to foreign security forces engaged in counterdrug activities to enhance their ability to conduct counterdrug operations and to stop the flow of illegal drugs into the United States
Developing Countries Combined Exercise Program	U.S.C. Title 10, §2010	The program provides funds for developing countries to participate in bilateral or multilateral exercises undertaken to enhance U.S. security interests
Disaster Response Training (Humanitarian Assistance)	U.S.C. Title 10, §2561	This training is provided by the U.S. military to enable the military of a host nation to improve its ability to respond effectively to disasters and thereby reduce or eliminate the need for a U.S. military response
Excess nonlethal supplies for humanitarian relief purposes	U.S.C. Title 10, §2557	OSD may provide excess nonlethal DoD supplies to foreign governments and civil organizations for humanitarian relief purposes when requested by the U.S. embassy
Foreign disaster assistance (Overseas Humanitarian Disaster Assistance and Civic Aid)	U.S.C. Title 10, §§402, 404, 2557, 2561	The program enables DoD to assist countries in their response to disasters when necessary to prevent the loss of life; services and supplies, logistical support, search and rescue, medical evacuation, and refugee assistance may be provided
Global Train and Equip Program	PL 109-163, §1206	The program enables DoD to conduct capacity-building programs with foreign military partners to improve their ability to conduct counterterrorist operations or support military and stability operations in areas that U.S. armed forces are also a participant

Table A.1—Continued

Program	Authority	Explanation of Program and Objectives
Humanitarian assistance transportation	U.S.C. Title 10, §2561	DoD provides transportation for humanitarian relief and other humanitarian purposes worldwide for nonprofit, nongovernment, and private volunteer organizations
Humanitarian and civic assistance in conjunction with military operations	U.S.C. Title 10, §§401, 407 DoDD 2205.2	Humanitarian and civic assistance activities may be carried out during authorized military operations if it is determined that the activity will promote the security interests of both the United States and the country in which the activities are to be carried out
Iraq security forces training (train and equip Iraqi security forces)	PL 109-364, §1516	The program allows DoD to provide equipment, supplies, services, and training to the Iraqi security forces to enable the Iraqi government to increase its counterinsurgency capabilities and assume greater responsibility for its security
Joint Combined Exchange Training Program	U.S.C. Title 10, §2011	The program authorizes U.S. special operations forces to conduct training overseas and exercise with foreign security forces to maintain readiness and to prepare for foreign operations and also meet the needs of the host nation
Lift and sustain (Iraq and Afghanistan)	PL 109-289, §9008	DoD is authorized to provide airlift and sustainment support at no cost to coalition partners participating in U.S. military operations in Iraq and Afghanistan to enable coalition countries to maintain their forces in Iraq and Afghanistan
Logistic support for allied forces participating in combined operations (global lift and sustain)	U.S.C. Title 10, §127c PL 109-364 §1201 PL 109-148 §9009	Logistic support is provided to allied forces participating in active hostilities, a contingency, or a noncombat operation alongside U.S. forces in a combined operation

Table A.1—Continued

Program	Authority	Explanation of Program and Objectives
Partnership for Peace Program (WIF)	U.S.C. Title 10, §§168, 1051, 2010 PL 108-375 §1224	The program assists newly independent states seeking cooperative military and peacekeeping relations with NATO by funding military contacts, bilateral or regional meetings, and combined exercises to advance closer relations and interoperability between NATO and these countries
Regional centers for security studies	U.S.C. Title 10, §§184, 1050, 1051 PL 109-364, §904 DoDD 5200.41	Five regional centers conduct courses and seminars on global and regional security for foreign military and civilian leaders in the United States and overseas to present U.S. foreign and defense policies and maintain communications with foreign leaders
Regional Defense CTFP	U.S.C. Title 10, §2249c PL 109-364 §1204	The CTFP enables foreign military officers and security officials in key partner nations to attend U.S. military educational institutions and selected regional centers for nonlethal training to build counterterrorism capabilities and increase cooperation in efforts to combat terrorism
Security and stabilization	PL 110-181, §1210 (formerly §1207)	The program enables OSD to provide services and defense articles to a foreign nation to facilitate the provision of reconstruction, security, and stabilization assistance
Transportation of humanitarian relief supplied to foreign counties (Denton Program)	U.S.C. Title 10, §402	The program authorizes the U.S. military to transport humanitarian relief supplies furnished by a nongovernmental source without charge on a space-available basis to foreign countries
Category 3: Title 22 Security Assistance and Other DOS-Managed Programs		
DCS	U.S.C. Title 22, §2778 Arms Export Control Act, §38	DCS allows eligible governments or international organizations to purchase defense articles or services directly from U.S. industry under a DOS-issued license

Table A.1—Continued

Program	Authority	Explanation of Program and Objectives
Distinguished Visitors Orientation Tours	U.S.C. Title 22, §2396 FAA §636(g)	These are short, intensive training programs designed to familiarize foreign military and civilian officials with U.S. security assistance courses and mobile training programs to initiate and strengthen relations with foreign militaries
Equipment leases	U.S.C. Title 22, §2796 AECA, §§61, 62 PL 90-269	Equipment leases enable the president to lease defense articles to friendly governments or international organizations for national security reasons to allow defense articles to be used for a short period (up to five years) at the lowest possible cost
Excess defense articles	U.S.C. Title 22, §§2321j, 2761 FAA §516 AECA §21	The program allows for the transfer of defense articles no longer needed by the U.S. armed forces to friendly (FMS-eligible) countries either by grant or by sale
Flight student exchanges	U.S.C. Title 22 FAA, §544b	The program authorizes no-cost reciprocal flight training
FMS	U.S.C. Title 22, §§2761, 2762, 2769, 2763; AECA §21, 22, 29	FMS enables eligible governments or organizations to purchase defense articles, services, or training from the U.S. government or contractors from DoD stocks or new procurements under DoD-managed contracts
FMF Program	U.S.C. Title 22, §2763–2394 PL 101-508 AECA, §§23, 24	This program provides grants and loans to eligible governments or organizations to purchase U.S.-produced equipment, services, and military training through the FMS Program or DCS to support U.S. regional stability goals and enable friends and allies to improve their defense capabilities
Global Peace Operations Initiative	U.S.C. Title 22, §§2348–2348d FAA §§551–554	The initiative is a five-year program in coordination with the other G-8 countries designed to increase peacekeeping capabilities in foreign countries, particularly Africa; the primary goals are to train 75,000 peace support troops and build a logistics system and training center

Table A.1—Continued

Program	Authority	Explanation of Program and Objectives
IMET	U.S.C. Title 22, §2347 FAA §§541–543, §622	The program provides training to military personnel from allied and friendly nations on a grant basis to improve defense capabilities, develop military-to-military relations, and promote democratic governance
International Narcotics Control and Law Enforcement Program	U.S.C. Title 22, §2291 FAA §§481–490	The program provides counternarcotics-related training to foreign military and law enforcement personnel to suppress the worldwide illicit manufacture and trafficking in narcotic drugs and to eliminate narcoterrorism
Loans of defense equipment	U.S.C. Title 22, §2796d AFI 16-110	Loans of defense equipment enable the United States to lend or borrow defense equipment or material without charge to or from NATO and major non-NATO allies for cooperative research, development, test, or evaluation
Reciprocal Training	U.S.C. Title 22, §2770a	Reciprocal training allows U.S. military units to train and support foreign units of friendly countries if the foreign country reciprocates with equivalent value training within one year

SOURCES: Defense Institute of Security Assistance Management, *Online Green Book: The Management of Security,* undated; Yvonne Eaton, "Distinguished Visitor Orientation Tour and Orientation Tour Program," *The DISAM Journal,* Fall 2003; GlobalSecurity.org, "US Military Exercises," undated; Major Derek I. Grimes, Major John Rawcliffe, and Captain Jeannine Smith, eds., *2006 Operational Law Handbook,* Judge Advocate General's Corps, 2006; Kenneth W. Martin, "Legislation for Fiscal Year 2008, *The DISAM Journal,* Vol. 30, No. 2, June 2008; W. Darrell Phillips, "Use of Operation and Maintenance Funds During Deployments," *Armed Forces Controller,* Fall 2006; U.S. Air Force, 1997b; U.S. Air Force, *US Air Force Participation in International Armaments Cooperation (IAC),* AFI 16-110, November 4, 2003b; U.S. Department of Defense, *Security Assistance Management Manual,* DoDD 5105.38-M, Chapter 10, October 3, 2003; U.S. Department of Defense, "Department of Defense Fiscal Year (FY) 2003 Budget Estimates and Justification," undated-b; U.S. Department of Defense, Office of the Under Secretary of Defense for Acquisition, Technology and Logistics, *International Armaments Cooperation Handbook, 4th ed.,* November 2006c; U.S. Department of State, "Foreign Military Training: Joint Report to Congress, Fiscal Years 2006 and 2007," Bureau of Political-Military Affairs, August 2007; U.S. Government Accountability Office, "Section 1206 Security Assistance Program: Findings on Criteria, Coordination, and Implementation," GAO-07-416R, February 28, 2007b.

Background on Case Studies

This appendix provides background information for the nine program case studies reviewed for this monograph and illustrated in Chapter Four. For each case, the following information is included: program stakeholder, objectives, processes in terms of how the program operates, resources, and any assessment activities that are currently ongoing. Table B.1 repeats the table found in Chapter Four showing the three categories of programs and the eight types of "ways."

Conferences, Seminars, and Workshops: Air Force Operator-to-Operator Talks

Stakeholder. Headquarters Air Force Regional Plans and Issues Division (HQ AF/A5XX). HQ AF/A5XX is the primary stakeholder for Air Force staff talks. These talks include CSAF counterpart visits, ops-to-ops talks, and airman-to-airman talks.

Objectives. The main objective of the program is to increase staff interoperability with select partner nations, which in turn can be linked to the AFGPS end state of building, sustaining, and expanding international relationships that are critical enablers for the Expeditionary Air and Space Force. Staff talks were instituted in 2000 and defined in a guidance memo signed by the AF/CV. The memo, entitled "International Engagement," specified seven countries with which the Air Force would conduct ops-to-ops talks. The group of participating countries changes and the decision to include or exclude a country

Table B.1
Case Studies, by Security Cooperation Way and Program Category

Way	Category 1: Title 10 Security Cooperation Programs Managed by the Air Force	Category 2: Title 10 Security Cooperation Programs Not Managed by the Air Force	Category 3: Title 22 Security Assistance Programs
Training			Canadian C-17 FMS
Education			IMET (AFIT)
Exercises		CJCS Exercise FLEXIBLE RESPONSE	
Exchanges	MPEP		
Conferences and workshops	UNIFIED ENGAGEMENT seminars		
Defense and military contacts	Ops-to-ops talks		
Equipment			Chile F-16 FMS, Canadian C-17 FMS Canadian C-17 DCS
Armaments cooperation		WGS SATCOM	

is typically made on recommendations by HQ AF/A5XX to the AF/CV. Since the talks began in 2000 with seven participating countries, talks with additional countries have been initiated and some have concluded. In 2008, 11 countries were included in the talks.[1] Typically, this indicates a maturing relationship, and other, often more substantive, security cooperation activities fill the gap when the staff talks are no longer conducted.

Processes. HQ AF/A5XX oversees the ops-to-ops talks, preparing agendas and invitations, arranging logistics, facilitating the discussions, and following up on action items that result from the talks. Despite not having a specific governing directive other than the

---

[1] Australia, Chile, France, Germany, Israel, Italy, Japan, the Netherlands, Singapore, South Korea, and the United Kingdom.

AF/CV memo, DoDD 5230.20, *Visits and Assignments of Foreign Nationals*, does address relevant aspects of managing such a program. In addition, AFIs are available that govern the routine management of O&M funds as well as Operational Representation Funds.

The talks take place on a rotating basis, with each country participating in talks approximately every 18 to 24 months. Five to six months before an event, HQ AF/A5XX solicits agenda inputs from the relevant COCOM, MAJCOM, SAF/IA, and Air Staff, as well as from the partner country. Agenda inputs form the basis for the discussions and are typically related to issues that can enhance the interoperability of the staffs. Other discussion items typically include other security cooperation programs, such as MPEP, training, and exercises. Once the agendas are completed, HQ AF/A5XX requests approval from the A3/A5. The U.S. Air Force delegations are led by an Air Force general officer and usually include one or two subject matter experts, a COCOM representative, a SAF/IA representative, and one officer from HQ AF/A5XX. Partner country delegations are similarly composed. The talks typically consist of a review of the status of any action items taken during previous talks, discussion of new agenda items, and agreement on any new action items. Other elements can include tours of relevant facilities, social events, and cultural tours.

Resources. There is no unique source of funding for the staff talks. Instead, they are funded through the normal O&M budget centrally maintained at the A3/A5 level. HQ AF/A5XX requests funding case by case, meaning that funding is allocated only as needed. In general, the funding covers only travel for the general officer leading the delegation and for one action officer from HQ AF/A5XX. Depending on the agenda, the funds also will cover the travel costs for one or two subject matter experts. All other participants, including those representing the partner countries, must cover their own expenses (i.e., they are not covered by the centrally maintained funds). In addition to travel, HQ AF/A5XX draws on ORF to pay for mementos and a portion of the dining and entertainment expenses.

Assessment Activity. Following the event, HQ AF/A5XX prepares a summary report that is routed to the CSAF and SAF for review.

In addition, HQ AF/A5XX updates A3/A5 on the status of any action items that result from the staff talks.

International Armaments Cooperation: Wideband Global Satellite Communications

Stakeholders. SAF/IA is the primary stakeholder for Air Force–related armaments cooperation programs. This role is largely connected to the establishment of the agreements but continues throughout the life of the program as SAF/IA monitors program activities.

Objectives. AFI 16-110 governs how the Air Force participates in IAC programs. The first paragraph of the instruction describes the program's purpose and objectives:

> The USAF participates in numerous IAC programs. Armaments cooperation applies to international requirements harmonization, research, development, test, evaluation, acquisition, production, and support of weapons and weapons-related technology. All USAF components should promote participation in international agreements with allied and friendly countries in support of the following objectives:
>
> - deploying and supporting common, or at least interoperable, equipment with U.S. friends and allies
> - achieving cost savings through cost-sharing and economies of scale afforded by coordinated research, development, production, and logistics support programs
> - pursuing the best technologies, military or civilian, available for equipping the United States, its allies, and other friendly nations
> - supplying the best available defense material to the United States, its allies, and other friendly nations in the most timely and cost-effective manner.[2]

Processes. WGS was originally conceived as a "gap-filler" system to bolster U.S. military secure SATCOM capability. The system archi-

---

[2]   U.S. Air Force, 2003b, p. 6.

tecture featured a five-satellite constellation, but a sixth was added as a result of a cooperative agreement with Australia. Australia had at first requested the SATCOM capability through the FMS process, but at the urging of SAF/IA, an International Cooperative Agreement Team was formed to consider whether a cooperative arrangement between the United States and Australia to use WGS might be preferable to providing Australia with a stand-alone capability.[3] The group developed funding and acquisition milestones, identified requirements for congressional notifications, and assessed various political and economic factors that might bear on the decision to proceed with the arrangement.

Operationally, the WGS spacecraft are flown by the Air Force's 3rd Space Operations Squadron at Schriever Air Force Base, Colorado. The spacecrafts' communications payloads are currently operated by the Army's Wideband Satellite Operations Center (WSOC) in Okinawa, Japan, and there is some discussion of potentially establishing a second WSOC in Australia. Since the WSOC operations crews comprise a mix of U.S. Army and Royal Australian Air Force personnel, this process is beyond the purview of the U.S. Air Force.

Resources. The Air Force was required to consider its sunk costs in the system as part of the U.S. contribution to the arrangement. These costs, in addition to the costs of the first five spacecraft, also included infrastructure, such as ground sensor stations and operations centers. As a result, the United States incurred no additional cost for adding the sixth satellite to the system, and Australia paid only for the incremental cost of adding the spacecraft. Ultimately, the Australians paid for approximately 11 percent of the overall cost of WGS and, in accordance with the cooperative agreement, will have access to 10 percent of the system's capacity. Much of the work to identify these sunk costs, as well as to identify the Australian share of the overall cost, was done by the Office of the Deputy Under Secretary of the Air Force for Space Acquisition.

---

[3] The team consisted of several offices, including SAF/IA, SAF/USA (space acquisition), and HQ AF/A3OS (space operations), as well representatives from AFSPC, U.S. Strategic Command, and the Army.

To complete the purchase of the sixth satellite, the Australian government provided funds to the Air Force Space and Missile Systems Center at Los Angeles Air Force Base, California. The Space and Missile Systems Center is the Air Force's acquisition center for all space systems, meaning that standard Air Force processes were used to acquire the satellite.

Assessment Activity. None.

Chairman of the Joint Chiefs of Staff Exercise: FLEXIBLE RESPONSE

Stakeholders. USAFE, as the air component command to EUCOM, is the primary Air Force stakeholder in this exercise. AFI 10-204, *Readiness Exercises and After-Action Reporting Program*, explains how the Air Force participates in exercises, including such combined exercises as FLEXIBLE RESPONSE.[4] USAFE, in its supplement to this instruction, assigns primary responsibility for planning and oversight of this participation to the Exercise Division (HQ USAFE/A3X). Within HQ USAFE/A3X, the Joint Exercise Branch (HQ USAFE/A3XJ) is the office responsible for overseeing the USAFE portion of FLEXIBLE RESPONSE. Much of the actual planning and development of the exercise, however, is conducted by 3 AF. The 3 AF/A9 leads this effort.

Objectives. FLEXIBLE RESPONSE is a CJCS exercise conducted annually by EUCOM. The focus of the exercise is on U.S. and partner responses to WMD attacks against EUCOM assets and, accordingly, one primary objective of FLEXIBLE RESPONSE is to exercise various agreements between the host nations and the U.S. military forces that cover their response to such attacks. For the most part, the responses are simply talked through in detail by U.S. and foreign military leaders, and the interaction between the affected sites is limited to commu-

---

[4] The term *combined* refers to military activity involving both the U.S. and foreign militaries.

nications between base command posts. This type of exercise is commonly referred to as a "command post exercise."

Processes. In the months leading up to the exercise, the Air Force stakeholders participate in planning conferences to help develop the exercise scenarios and objectives. In 2008, the exercise consisted of several separate but related scenarios, including four at USAFE bases in Germany and Italy. At Landstuhl Air Base, Germany, the exercise participants responded to a scenario involving a radiological dispersal device, simulated high explosives were detonated at Vogelweh Air Base several miles to the east, and further south in the Bavarian Alps, an outbreak of plague was unleashed at Garmisch, home to the George C. Marshall European Center for Security Studies. In Italy, Aviano Air Base was dealt a simulated attack with chemical weapons.

For the FLEXIBLE RESPONSE 2008, USAFE decided to go a step beyond the CPX nature of the exercise. With the support of the 3 AF Vice Commander, 3 AF/A9 built on the existing scenario and developed an internal USAFE exercise to be conducted during FLEXIBLE RESPONSE. The idea was to add realism by requiring that the 31st Fighter Wing at Aviano Air Base simulate its actions in response to the simulated chemical attack. Much of this would include communicating with 3 AF and simulating the deployment of first responders and other follow-on actions to mitigate the consequences of the attack. One outside observer, the Defense Threat Reduction Agency, objected to this spin-off of the main exercise, suggesting that it was too far removed from the main objectives of FLEXIBLE RESPONSE 2008 and might detract from its execution. USAFE continued despite this and successfully completed the "Air Force–only" exercise in a way that was largely transparent to EUCOM and others participating.

Resources. Although USAFE and 3 AF participation in planning conferences for the exercise is funded by the Joint Staff, the resources for the actual execution in the exercise are simply O&M funds. In a CPX such as FLEXIBLE RESPONSE, the primary Air Force resources used are essentially the time and effort contributed by the assigned airmen. This was also true for the "Air Force–only" exercise between Aviano Air Base and 3 AF.

Assessment Activity. Assessments of CJCS exercises may be conducted using the routine procedures prescribed by CJCSM 3500.03, *Joint Training Manual for the Armed Forces of the United States*, and CJCSI 3150.05, *Chairman of the Joint Chiefs of Staff Assessment Program*. The procedures require that COCOMs nominate a representative sample of exercises for assessment each year. In addition, lessons learned are provided routinely using the procedures prescribed in CJCSI 3150.25, *Joint Lessons Learned Program*. These procedures require that the COCOMs submit lessons learned from exercises and other training activities in a standardized way, so that, among other things, they can be used to inform the development of future exercises of a similar nature. USAFE, as the air component command to EUCOM, participates in this process. It is interesting to note that even though EUCOM was not involved in the "Air Force–only" exercise between Aviano Air Base and 3 AF, the lessons learned from that exercise were forwarded to EUCOM along with the main FLEXIBLE RESPONSE lessons learned, making them available to future exercise planners.

Exchanges: The Military Personnel Exchange Program

Stakeholders. Although SAF/IA is the primary stakeholder for the Air Force MPEP, other Air Force stakeholders include the component commands and a number of regional PMOs and CONUS PMOs.[5] MPEP also has external stakeholders, including the in-country SAO and the COCOMs.

---

[5]   The five regional PMOs are Air Force Elements Personnel Exchange Program (AFELM/ PEP) Canada (Canada); AFELM/PEP Europe (Europe, Middle East, and Africa); HQ PACAF Plans and Programs Office (Asia-Pacific); and 474 OG/PEP (Latin America). The 11 CONUS PMOs are AETC/IAD (supports AETC Foreign Disclosure Office); AMC/A5 (supports Air Mobility Command); AFSAC/IAS (supports AFMC); ACC/A3TS (supports Air Combat Command); AFSOC/A2S (supports Air Force Special Operations Command); HQ AFSPC/A8IF (supports Headquarters Air Force Space Command Foreign Disclosure Branch); PACAF/XP (supports Pacific Air Forces); USAFA/DFIP (supports the U.S. Air Force Academy); 162 OG/CCI (supports the 162nd Fighter Wing, Arizona ANG); and

Objectives. According to AFI 16-107, *Military Personnel Exchange Program*, Air Force MPEP is intended to

- promote mutual understanding and trust
- enhance interoperability through mutual understanding of doctrine, tactics, techniques, and procedures of both air forces and strengthen air force–to–air force ties
- develop long-term professional and personal relationships.

These objectives can in turn be linked to the AFGPS end state of building, sustaining, and expanding international relationships that are critical enablers for the Expeditionary Air and Space Force.

Processes. SAF/IA generally coordinates the selection and assignment of exchange officers, both U.S. Air Force and foreign. Recommendations for these exchanges are provided by the air component commands. The regional PMOs are responsible for the day-to-day administrative support of U.S. Air Force officers assigned in their region. This includes ensuring that the officers are paid, that their performance is evaluated, and that any other logistical or administrative needs are taken care of. Additional support is provided by the SAO when needed. On the other hand, the CONUS PMOs are responsible for similar activities in support of foreign officers assigned to U.S. Air Force units. For example, 474 OG/PEP at Davis-Monthan Air Force Base hosts the CONUS PMO responsible for the day-to-day oversight of foreign exchange officers assigned to the SOUTHCOM AOR. Similarly, the 162nd Fighter Wing, also at Davis-Monthan Air Force Base, has a CONUS PMO to support foreign students assigned to the unit as pilot instructors.

Resources. The MPEP budget funds the expenses of U.S. Air Force officers assigned to a foreign military. It also covers the cost of operating the regional PMOs and CONUS PMOs. The foreign exchange officer's nation is responsible for his or her expenses while

---

NGB/SPP (supports the National Guard Bureau). SAF/IA (Airmen Division) supports Field Operating Agencies and HQ Air Force Direct Reporting Units. U.S. Air Force, 2006a.

assigned to the program. FMS or IMET is not used to fund participation in MPEP.

Assessment Activity. MPEP selections can provide insight into the success of other Air Force security cooperation activities. For example, the Air Force officer recently selected for the exchange assignment with Chile was chosen because of his background in F-16 logistics and maintenance. Because the F-16 FMS case with Chile was structured in a way that provided only limited insight into how Chile uses and maintains the aircraft, this exchange has the potential to provide the Air Force valuable feedback that could be used to improve and enhance future sales.

Seminars: UNIFIED ENGAGEMENT Building Partner Capacity Regional Seminars

Stakeholders. HQ AF/A5XS is the primary stakeholder for UNIFIED ENGAGEMENT BPC regional seminars. During the planning phase, HQ AF/A5XS coordinates with SAF/IA and HQ AF/A5XX, as well as the COCOMs and component commands, to develop seminar agendas and identify subject matter experts for possible participation.

Objectives. The objective of the UNIFIED ENGAGEMENT seminars is probably best linked to the AFGPS end state of building, sustaining, and expanding international relationships that are critical enablers for the Expeditionary Air and Space Force. The seminars are not governed by any directives, and the sole responsibility for their content lies with the primary stakeholder, HQ AF/A5XS. As mentioned above, other stakeholders do have an opportunity during the planning phase to shape the objectives. For example, USAFE now has started to ensure that the activities they recommend are linked to the EUCOM Strategy for Active Security and the GEF.

Processes. HQ AF/A5XS conducts several unclassified seminars each year with a variety of partners. This seminar program is somewhat disconnected from the major Air Force war game UNIFIED ENGAGEMENT because that war game is conducted at a classified level and does not include foreign participants. In contrast, "jointness" is a key component of each seminar. In a recent seminar conducted in Bucharest, Romania, HQ AF/A5XS involved U.S. Army Europe and Special Operations Command Europe and tried, unsuccessfully, to include the U.S. Naval Command Europe and U.S. Marine Forces Europe as participants as well. The 3 AF was also invited but chose not to participate. Because of its proximity, USAFE was able to coordinate host-nation support and also engage directly with other participating countries to facilitate their participation.

Resources. UNIFIED ENGAGEMENT is funded through normal O&M funding, budgeted for annually as an HQ AF/A5XS activity. EUCOM provided approximately $40,000 in TCA funds. The TCA funded travel expenses for all foreign participants in the event, including their airfare, hotel, and meals, but not their per diems. In addition, ORFs were used to cover the expense of food and drink during the social events. The primary Air Force resource was the time and effort of the HQ AF/A5XS personnel and the subject matter experts from elsewhere on the Air Staff or from the COCOM or its components. In a recent UNIFIED ENGAGEMENT seminar that focused its agenda on irregular warfare, for example, a staff officer from U.S. Army Europe was brought in to assist with the discussion.

Assessment Activity. None.

Equipment Transfer Direct Commercial Sale Case: Canadian C-17 Sale

Stakeholders. In early July 2006, the Canadian government announced that it was buying four C-17 Globemaster III transport aircraft from Boeing for approximately $3.4 billion, of which about $1.6 billion was for a 20-year maintenance agreement with Boeing. The primary Air Force stakeholders for this program are SAF/IA, AFMC, and the AFSAC.

Objectives. DCS must be consistent with U.S. laws governing the sale of military articles to foreign countries.

Processes. Air Force involvement in DCS cases is minimal and is generally limited to ensuring that the sale complies with U.S. law. This also means that the Air Force will have only limited insight into how the foreign partner will use the equipment and limited influence over the type of equipment purchased. However, the Air Force can gain this type of insight by offering an attractive FMS support case. This is precisely what the Air Force did with the Canadian C-17 sale, enabling the Air Force to work closely with the Canadians on training, maintenance, sustainment, and operational issues related to the employment of the C-17 aircraft. Although the actual FMS case will be discussed in greater detail in the next section, one aspect of that case is inextricably linked to the DCS.

The 516 AESG is the Air Force's C-17 SPO. The group is responsible for all aspects of C-17 system acquisition and sustainment and is organized to do this not only for the U.S. Air Force but also for partner countries, such as the United Kingdom, Australia, and Canada. One tool that the 516 AESG uses to carry out its responsibilities is its GSP contract with Boeing. The GSP is a contractor logistics support contract that it is designed to ensure that the Air Force has access to spare parts, necessary repairs, and engineering support for the aircraft. In fact, under the GSP, Boeing even manages the supply chain for C-17 parts, providing warehousing, shipping, and parts management.

In the case of the direct commercial sale of C-17s from Boeing to Canada, the 516 AESG was able to leverage the GSP to develop an attractive companion FMS case. Although not technically part of the DCS case, the 516 AESG was aware that many of the items necessary for the production of the Canadian aircraft were already available as spare parts under the GSP. By providing a number of items back to Boeing as government-furnished equipment, the overall cost of the DCS could be reduced. Canada agreed and, in conjunction with the DCS case, it initiated an FMS that included the purchase of these spare parts from the U.S. Air Force. The parts were then transferred to Boeing by the 516 AESG and used in the subsequent production of the four Canadian C-17s. This included 18 engines as well as about 80 to 100 additional items, including such defensive systems as the Large Aircraft Infrared Countermeasures system, Global Positioning System equipment, flares, classified COMSEC equipment, ground support equipment, and palletized seating.

Resources. Although the Air Force uses no resources directly in support of the DCS case, some effort is made to conduct technical transfer compliance reviews. Moreover, the 516 AESG was engaged in learning the details of the case and developing an approach that allowed it to effectively link a large FMS case to it.

Assessment Activity. Although there is no direct assessment activity for this case, it will give the Air Force a way to gain insight into the overall effectiveness of the Canadian C-17 sale.

Equipment Transfer and Training Foreign Military Sales Case: Support for Canadian C-17s

Stakeholders. Although Canada purchased four C-17s through a direct commercial sale, it purchased support and training through an FMS case supported by the Air Force. The C-17 training was designed for both the aircrews and for the maintenance technicians. Stakeholders in this effort include SAF/IA, HQ AETC, HQ AMC, AFSAC, the 516 AESG, AFSAT, the 97 AMW, and Detachment 5 of the 373 TRS.

Objectives. As described above, the 516 AESG is the SPO responsible for acquisition and sustainment of the Air Force's C-17 transport aircraft. In addition, the group also manages C-17-related security assistance cases and is the primary stakeholder in the equipment transfer portion of the case. The primary tool used by the unit is the GSP contract with Boeing. Boeing, under this Contractor Logistics Support contract, performs some functions traditionally done by Air Force organizations, such as managing the supply chain for all parts and spares that are unique to the C-17. To use the GSP to support the Canadian C-17 sales case, the 516th Canada IPT prepared an amendment to the contract that specified exactly which services Boeing would provide. In this way, the majority of the objectives are defined contractually.

A great deal of coordination was required to develop the objectives and plan the training. In particular, AFSAT coordinated with AETC and with the Canadian armed forces to establish objectives for the training. AFSAT coordinated with 19th Air Force to develop the flying training curriculum and with HQ AETC/A3 to develop the technical training curriculum. The process for allocating flying training slots for international partners is the International Flying Training Board. AFSAT, in coordination with SAF/IA and HQ AF/A3OT (Operations Training), prioritizes the requests for flying. In this process, SAF/IA makes the final decision as to which countries will get the available flying training slots. For the technical training, AETC officials participated in a number of planning meetings organized by AFSAT. These meetings also included Canadian participants. It was through these meetings that training managers and subject matter experts developed course objectives for the proposed curriculum, identified the locations and materials required, and prepared schedules for the courses.[6]

Processes. At the beginning of the case, SAF/IA performs functions that contribute to the compliance with various aspects of U.S. law related to the transfer of military equipment. In this particular case, AFSAC personnel worked closely with AFSAT, AETC, AMC, and others to finalize the support and training case. DSCA does call on AFSAC case managers for their expertise in Air Force systems and as well as their contributions to the case development. In this way, Air Force security assistance planners gain insight into the case requirements and can begin to prepare for the case.

In the C-17 FMS case, the 516 AESG established the Canada IPT to handle activities related to the program. The Canada IPT comprises Air Force civilian and military personnel, including a warranted contracting office, a financial management analyst, a budgeting officer, and acquisition and logistics professionals. In addition, four Canadian military personnel are assigned to the office to facilitate interaction with the Royal Canadian Air Force. For the most part, the 516 AESG manages the day-to-day execution of the case with little involvement by AFSAC. AFSAC case managers typically manage systems that are common to multiple systems, or in some cases they manage older, more established systems, such as the F-16. As a result, AFSAC personnel have sometimes assisted with obtaining parts or supplies that are not unique to the C-17.

---

[6]   Travel expenses for participation in these meetings were funded by the FMS case. Discussion with AETC official, June 2008.

Another example of interaction between the SPO and AFSAC is the modification of contracts. Although the 516 AESG has a contracting officer assigned, modifications to contracts are reviewed and approved by personnel at AFSAC. At the end of the case, however, the expectation is that many aspects of the follow-on case will be handled by AFSAC case managers. This is typical and reflects the maturation of the system and the increasing commonality of its parts with those of other systems.[7]

SAF/IA also is engaged with the program and focuses on activities that are more high-level than day-to-day case management. These activities can include the preparation of agreements, leases, and other arrangements that help to facilitate the execution of the case. For example, when an item of ground support equipment (a heavy forklift loader) was unavailable to support the case, SAF/IA arranged to have the Air Force lease one to the Canadian government. The item was designed specifically for the C-17 but was no longer available commercially. SAF/IA was able to work with HQ AMC to arrange for two of the loaders to be leased to the Canadians for two years.

A second major piece of the FMS case was to provide training to Canadian aircrew members and maintenance technicians. The flying training was conducted by the 97 AMW at Altus Air Force Base, Oklahoma, and consisted of ground school, simulator training, and actual time flying the C-17 aircraft. The ground school and simulator portion was conducted by contractor personnel, but this was normal for all C-17 flying training and was not unique to the Canadian case. The flying portion was conducted by U.S. Air Force flying instructors using standard training procedures common to all U.S. Air Force flying training.

Technical training for the maintenance technicians is more specialized and was designed as a unique program for the Canadians. The training was conducted by AETC's Detachment 5 of the 373 TRS at Charleston Air Force Base, South Carolina, an AMC C-17 base.

---

[7] The case was established in 2007 and will close in 2012. One example given by an 516 AESG official was that if the follow-on air refueling aircraft were produced by Boeing, then there would likely be a number of parts in common with the C-17.

Detachment 5 reports to its parent unit, the 373 TRS, at Sheppard Air Force Base, Texas. Management of the training, therefore, is done by the 373 TRS and, accordingly, the squadron training manager is AFSAT's main point of contact for this case. Although Detachment 5 is tasked with training the Canadian technicians, it also trains U.S. Air Force technicians. Training of the Canadian students, however, became AETC's first priority, somewhat to the consternation of the AMC personnel assigned to the U.S. Air Force C-17 unit.[8]

Part of the training effort included modifying the U.S. curriculum to fit the Canadian concept for maintaining the aircraft. The U.S. curriculum trains seven separate specialties for C-17 maintenance, but the Canadians decided to consolidate that to two: avionics specialists and mechanics specialists. This decision required that the United States consolidate its curriculum similarly. Throughout the process, AFSAT remained the "face to the customer," taking the proposals to the Canadians and serving as the interlocutor between them and the U.S. trainers and subject matter experts.

AFSAT and AETC also worked with AMC to incorporate "seasoning" training for the Canadians. Once the Canadian technicians completed the AETC course, they stayed on at Charleston Air Force Base to work under the supervision of U.S. C-17 maintenance technicians assigned to the operational C-17 unit. In doing, so, the new technicians received hands-on experience under the mentorship of veteran technicians. To ensure that this OJT would meet Canadian requirements, AFSAT and AETC training managers met with counterparts from HQ AMC to develop the program and agree on its structure. As the number of qualified and experienced C-17 technicians in the Royal Canadian Air Force grows, the seasoning training will shift from AMC to the Canadian base at Trenton, Ontario. Similarly, over time, the responsibility for instructing some elements of the technical training course is being shifted from Detachment 5 to the Canadian Air Force.

During the planning stages for the case, the 516 AESG also recognized the need for training Canadian aircrew members and mainte-

---

[8] AFI 36-2201 provided the guidance to make the international students the top priority (U.S. Air Force, 2002).

nance technicians on certain unique equipment that had been provided to Boeing for the production of the aircraft. After coordinating with personnel at AFSAT, the 516 AESG confirmed that these items would not be part of the flying training or technical training conducted by AETC. As a result, the 516 AESG arranged for this training to take place through a variety of sources. One interesting example was the training provided for the Automated Air Load Planning System, which is used to calculate the best way to load personnel and equipment onto a transport aircraft. Because the Army is a major user of Air Force airlift capability, AALPS is managed by the U.S. Army's Transportation Information Systems PMO. As a result, the 516 AESG arranged for the Army to deploy a team to Trenton to train the Canadian aircrew and ground support personnel to use the system.

Resources. Detachment 5 was selected for the training because of the training resources already at its disposal. The unit has access to a number of training devices, including engines and other major aircraft components, as well as mock-ups of aircraft systems.[9] To ensure that the detachment had the right mix of skills to conduct the training, AETC arranged to have instructors from other bases reassigned to Charleston Air Force Base to augment the unit's expertise. Some of these instructors were permanently assigned. However, some of the additional instructors were assigned only temporarily and returned to their home bases after the program was firmly established. As the detachment at Charleston began preparing for its role as the primary unit for training Canadian C-17 technicians, the training detachment at McChord Air Force Base, Washington, which had previously trained Australian C-17 maintenance technicians under a separate sales case, briefly provided some of the expertise and initial training for the Canadians.[10] With the Detachment 5 program fully under way, the throughput of students is approximately six avionics technicians and six mechanics per year.

---

[9] These training devices were purchased by AMC for AETC to use during training of AMC C-17 maintenance technicians.

[10] Two AETC field training detachments are collocated with operational U.S. Air Force C-17 units.

At the 516 AESG as well as with other stakeholders such as SAF/IA and AFSAC, those positions that directly support the Canadian C-17 program are funded through the FMS case on a reimbursable basis.

Assessment Activity. Training activities are documented using standard AETC processes, and those successfully finishing the technical training program receive a certificate of completion. Seasoning training is documented by the OJT supervisor in a ledger maintained by the trainee. Periodically, personnel from the Royal Canadian Air Force Headquarters in Winnipeg, Manitoba, meet with AETC, AFSAT, and AMC personnel to review the program's progress. This forum not only allows the U.S. Air Force to discuss issues of interest, but it also gives the Canadians the opportunity to provide feedback regarding the quality of the training. Finally, as a matter of standard AETC practice, a review of the entire course is conducted every two years to determine if it is still meeting its objectives. In particular, this exchange should be of keen interest to AMC given that Canadian C-17s are now available to augment U.S. C-17s.

Assessment of the equipment transfer activities is primarily accomplished by the 516 AESG through its quality assurance surveillance of the GSP contract. In addition, AFSAC conducts a semiannual review of all major FMS programs. This review, known as the International Acquisition, Sustainment, and Training Review, draws on relevant data from the various contract surveillance plans and the assessment process-oriented activities, such as the timeliness of case closure. These data are then summarized in a series of "stop light" charts that indicate the relative status of the program. Participants in the review include AFSAC, the SPO, SAF/IA, AETC/IA, and AFSAT.

Equipment Transfer Foreign Military Sales Case Funded by Foreign Military Financing: Support for Chilean F-16s

Stakeholders. In 2006, Chile purchased the LAU-129A missile launcher rail for firing AIM-9 and AIM-120 air-launched missiles from F-16 fighter aircraft.[11] As with most FMS cases, major U.S. Air Force stakeholders include SAF/IA, HQ AETC, HQ AMC, AFSAT, and AFSAC.

Objectives. Because this rail is similar to the rail used by the U.S. Air Force, AFSAT facilitated a training contract with Lockheed-Martin to conduct the training at their facilities in Fort Worth, Texas. Training objectives aimed at ensuring that maintenance technicians and pilots were able to properly use the missile launcher rail and were included in the contract statement of work.

Processes. The training consisted of classroom instruction and hands-on training using the actual rail system. In addition, Lockheed-Martin conducted some follow-on training in Chile to address some of the specialized aspects of the Chilean system.

The acquisition of the rail is managed by AFSAC. The AFSAC case manager coordinated procurement and delivery of the rail launcher systems with the item manager at the Ogden Air Logistics Center in Utah.

Resources. Training and equipment were funded by the FMS case, as were the personnel positions for those involved in the case. Because this was a relatively small case, this case alone could not completely fund these positions. In such events, the Air Force aggregates multiple, similar cases to determine how many case managers are required.

Assessment Activity. Because the training is conducted by contractors, AFSAT developed a quality assurance program to gain insight into how well Lockheed-Martin performed the training. This program included a regular self-assessment prepared by the contractor as well site visits by AFSAT personnel to the contractor facility to observe the training in progress. AFSAT program managers also reviewed student

---

[11] The rail launcher is affixed to the wing of the aircraft, and a missile is then attached to it. When the missile is launched, the rail serves to guide the missile in a steady direction until it has cleared the aircraft and is guided by its own, internal navigation system.

feedback forms to identify any problems or negative trends in the quality of the training.

Education: International Military Education and Training Students at the Air Force Institute of Technology

Stakeholders. The AFIT offers graduate degrees (master's and Ph.D.s) in nearly 30 technical disciplines. Each year, approximately 20–25 international students participate in AFIT degree programs. IMET funds may be used to pay for the attendance of foreign students. SAF/IA, AFSAT, HQ AETC, Air University, and AFIT are the major Air Force stakeholders in this program. In addition, DSCA, the COCOMs, and the applicable security assistance officers are involved in various aspects of the program.

Objectives. International students attending AFIT participate in a standard educational course designed for U.S. Air Force officers, earning an advanced degree in a discipline agreed on by both the U.S. Air Force and the partner country.

Processes. Students are nominated for attendance by the partner country, but a thorough review by several U.S. stakeholders is completed before the student is accepted into the program. This process is documented in Air Force Joint Instruction 16-105, *Joint Security Assistance Training.*[12] When a country requests a specific degree, AFIT works primarily with external stakeholders, such as DSCA and the security assistance officer, to ensure that the potential student is qualified for the program. This is an essential process, as the advanced degrees are often highly technical (i.e., covering mathematics, engineering, and physics), and the courses are taught only in English. In addition to this case-specific interaction, AFIT participates in each COCOM's annual training program management reviews, which are designed to review the various international training requirements. Participants typically include representatives from the COCOM staffs, security assistance

---

[12] The Air Force, Army, and Navy all use the same instruction, but each service has a different designation for it. U.S. Air Force, undated-a.

officers, DSCA, the affected academic institutions, and the partner countries.

IMET students at AFIT use the same facilities and instructors as U.S. students and take the same courses. The major difference for these students is the specialized International Student Management Office (IMSO) that was created to assist them and ensure that U.S. obligations under the IMET agreement are being fulfilled. IMSO interfaces periodically with Air University to ensure that its programs are in compliance with their policies. Air University Instruction 16-102, *International Programs,* describes these requirements. IMSO works routinely with AFSAT and the applicable security assistance officers to ensure that student and program needs are met.

Resources. AFIT is reimbursed through the FMF accounts for the attendance of international students, meaning that there is no actual control of funds. This reimbursement activity is handled by the financial management community, much like any other transfer of funds from one organization to another, and so is essentially transparent to the program managers.

Assessment Activity. Because IMET students participate in standard courses offered to U.S. students, routine surveys and feedback are collected to help refine courses and develop new courses. AFSAT and DSCA recently created an automated program to collect feedback from students participating in IMET programs, including IMET students at AFIT. Additionally, AFIT is required to participate in DSCA's annual security cooperation assessment. In addition, given that IMET students selected to attend U.S. courses often rise to senior rank and assume key positions in their respective air forces, consideration should be given to developing an assessment process for IMET to assess the effects on air force–to–air force relationships and how Air University and AFIT courses could be modified and improved.

Assessment Examples

This appendix provides examples to illustrate how the Air Force might assess the need for a program and its design and theory. The examples are not exhaustive but represent our best efforts to suggest what might be involved: the actors, the data, the processes, and the outcomes that would be necessary to mobilize assessments to support decisions confronting Air Force security cooperation stakeholders. Each example below describes the decisions that security cooperation assessments might be called on to support, the process of organizing that support, and an example of how the events might unfold in a specific, Air Force–managed, security cooperation program.

Need for the Program

Questions about the need for a given program stand at the top of the hierarchy of evaluation. Decisions here have to do with whether to continue the program, to increase or decrease its size, or to cancel it.

Decision Context

Questions about the continuing need for a program might arise in the face of increasing budget pressures, the QDR, or some other strategic review mandated by a new administration or perhaps by new leaders within DoD.

The Air Force's contribution could be to formulate a recommendation and to forward it, with appropriate supporting documentation (i.e., relevant program assessments and analysis). Given that many Air

Force security cooperation programs have long histories and often several antecedent programs, decisions on the need for a program are relatively rare and, therefore, would probably be sent to OSD over the signatures of the CSAF or SAF, or both.

Process of Organizing Support

To launch an effort to reach a recommendation about the need for an Air Force security cooperation program, the service would embark on a lengthy process involving seven steps:

1. tasking Air Force organizations to help collect data, conduct assessments, and validate and integrate results
2. collecting relevant information on the question, which could include both expert views from senior officials and data bearing (both directly and indirectly) on the question
3. assessing the program in question and conducting analysis of the results to gain insights into the need for the program
4. validating the results of those assessments
5. integrating the results of the assessments to shed light on the question of the need for the program
6. formulating a recommendation that is consistent with the facts in evidence
7. staffing the recommendation up the chain of command.

Example: The Aviation Leadership Program

According to Chapter 905, U.S.C. Title 10, "the Air Force may establish and maintain an Aviation Leadership Program to provide undergraduate pilot training and necessary related training to personnel of the air forces of friendly, less-developed foreign nations . . . (which) . . . furthers the interests of the United States, promotes closer relations with such nations, and advances the national security."[1] Given the expectations for the program found in Title 10 of the U.S. Code, the question of the need for the program hinges on whether the evidence indicates

---

[1]   Aviation Leadership Program, 10 U.S. Code, Chapter 905, January 8, 2008.

that the program has produced the expected benefits—that is, closer relations have developed between the United States and the program's participants and U.S. national security has benefited from these relationships. Other benefits that the legislation did not anticipate might influence senior leaders' view of the need for the program. Of course, there are also problems of causality—actually demonstrating that the Aviation Leadership Program was responsible for closer relations and improved U.S. national security—given that other international programs are also under way and might affect the same countries.

The Air Force needs to take at least seven steps when evaluating the need for this program. First, the service must task its subordinates to help with the assessment. It might turn to its Air Attachés serving in the participating countries for insights and historical data revealing trends in U.S.-participant relations. Likewise, it might task the relevant numbered Air Force to discover general tendencies in U.S.-participant country relations, frictions, and attitudes among their airmen, and similar data. Aviation Leadership Program managers might also discover trends that suggest the state of affairs in their reports and administrative documents: numbers of participants over time, exit interviews, end-of-tour reports, and similar reporting that might reveal a growing appreciation of U.S. policies and security perspectives over the years on the part of participating countries. Air Force intelligence could contribute as well, providing country assessments and other time-series data that might reveal correlations between periods of intensive involvement in the Aviation Leadership Program and cordial relations and supportive policies between the participating countries and the United States.

The second step would be to assemble and organize the information. For long-lived programs, such as the Aviation Leadership Program, ten-year, time-series data might be appropriate.[2] How might we expect these data to appear at tactical unit and program level? A search for indications of closer relations may require indirect evidence: trends that reveal an increase in enrollments or requests for quotas to par-

---

[2] Although these data are very difficult to acquire unless the Air Force anticipates the data requirements of the hierarchy of evaluation and directs the appropriate constituent organizations to collect and maintain them.

ticipate in the program, trends in flight and leadership proficiency,[3] or perhaps trends in interoperability (participation is a definite indication of participants' desire to fly with the U.S. Air Force). Thus, such trends might be treated as proxies for the outcomes anticipated by the legislation that established the program. Data that could allow the Air Force to document these trends might be found in attaché reporting, in reports on exercises and competitions (e.g., numbers of participants from different countries), from intelligence briefs and assessments, and from program managers' assessments.

The third step would be to perform the program assessments. The assessments involve three types of tasks: (1) collecting the views of senior leaders on the benefits of the program, (2) organizing the raw data extracted from the reports and sources mentioned in the paragraph above using statistical methods to understand the relationship between program activities and the resulting changes in relationships between the participant countries and the United States, and (3) determining the relative cost-effectiveness of the program.[4] Critics may dismiss the views of senior leaders as anecdotes, but that would be a misperception; their views are better seen as field observations taken from subject matter experts. Senior leaders often enjoy broader perspectives and can thus appreciate a security cooperation program in a context that would not be obvious to program managers. The statistical analysis would measure quantitatively whether intensification of a partner's involvement in the Aviation Leadership Program correlates with the benefits to the United States anticipated in Air Force doctrine and instructions: an improvement in relations with the partner country, advancement of

---

[3] On the notion that participants would not emulate and seek to perfect the practices of an air force of a country it despised.

[4] Common statistical methods that may be relevant for analysis in support of assessments include, for example, pre-test–post-test trend analysis, linear or multivariate regression analysis, and the analysis of covariance. For examples of detailed discussions of the use of statistical methods, see David Draper, James S. Hodges, Edward E. Leamer, Carl N. Morris, and Donald B. Rubin, *A Research Agenda for Assessment and Propagation of Model Uncertainty,* Santa Monica, Calif.: RAND Corporation, N-2683-RC, 1987, and Bernice B. Brown, *Delphi Process: A Methodology Used for the Elicitation of Opinions,* Santa Monica, Calif.: RAND Corporation, P-3925, 1968.

U.S. national interests, and an improvement in U.S. national security. Program managers might be able to establish basic cost-per-output figures for the program, but the Air Force would probably need a service-level entity—a PA&E-like organization—with comprehensive cost data to compare the relative cost-effectiveness of the program with all other Air Force programs, including those outside the domain of security cooperation. In other words, determining the need for the program might involve considering the value of the program relative to other programs. Would the Air Force and the United States benefit more in improved foreign relations and national security through the Aviation Leadership Program or some other program?

Next, the results of the assessments must be validated and integrated—perhaps by SAF/IA, as this monograph suggests. Validation would require a review of the assessment data, the way the trends were constructed, the sources of the cost data, and the consistency of views among the senior leaders asked about the program. Integration of assessment results would involve discovering consistencies and patterns among them that may help the Air Force reach conclusions about what the Aviation Leadership Program is and is not delivering over the course of years.[5]

This validated, integrated assessment should allow us to form a view of what Aviation Leadership is and is not accomplishing over time, including unanticipated effects, both negative and positive, and to establish the relative cost-effectiveness of the program. Thus equipped, we can move on to step six, and formulate a recommendation concerning the need for the program.

Based on the analysis that indicates the program is relatively cost-effective compared with other Air Force programs, we could forward a recommendation to retain it. However, if the analysis does not support a recommendation to retain the program, then there is more work to be done. For example, if the program's relative cost-effectiveness stacks up poorly against all other programs, the Air Force would probably want to pay special attention to the context in which the question was

---

[5] It may be important to avoid the temptation to view recent events as separate and decoupled from the deeper past and concentrate on what the long-term trends reveal.

raised. If it results from increased budget pressures, for example, then that fact might drive the service to recommend reducing or canceling the program. Likewise, if the analysis reveals that the hoped-for results from the Aviation Leadership Program are not in evidence, this might lead the Air Force to recommend canceling the program.

The seventh and final step involves staffing the recommendation up the chain of command. The staffing process provides opportunities for other stakeholders to weigh in on the recommendation for the future of the Aviation Leadership Program. Assuming that the recommendation survives the staffing process, it would make its way to the SAF and CSAF who would sign off on it and forward it to OSD.

Assessment of Design and Theory

Questions surrounding the design and theory of a security cooperation program center on "does it work as advertised?" Is it reasonable to expect, given the program's inputs and process, that it would produce the results we expect from it?

Decision Context

Assessment of design and theory is implicit in some Air Force and DoDIs that require periodic assessments of security cooperation programs. In the example examined here, the Defense Research, Development, Test and Evaluation IEP, DoDI 2015.4, requires such an assessment.[6] Questions concerning the robustness of a program's design and theory could also emerge from budget pressures such as those described in the first example in this appendix, or from officials interested in determining where to make additional investments.

DoDI 2015.4 calls for "periodic bilateral and multilateral reviews of IEPs with partner nations to coordinate their management," and "periodic internal reviews of IEPs including assessment of desirability

---

[6] Office of the Under Secretary of Defense (Acquisition, Technology and Logistics), DoDI 2015.4, February 7, 2002.

of revising or terminating . . . (those) inactive or that lack significant activity."[7]

Process of Organizing Support

As was the case with our first example, the Air Force also faces a multistep process for assessing the design and theory of its IEP. The steps might include the following:

1. task subordinate Air Force organizations for assistance
2. identify and test the logical consistency of the assumptions about the design and theory of the program
3. gather time-series data for 5 to ten years[8] across all the available IEPs[9]
4. conduct an empirical test to determine whether program results comport with expectations
5. perform the assessments
6. validate the results
7. integrate the results
8. formulate a recommendation
9. staff the recommendation up the chain of command.

Example: The Defense Research, Development, Test and Evaluation Information Exchange Program

As noted, it is expected that the program's information exchanges will promote additional technical cooperation, improve multinational force compatibility, and promote equitable access to scientific-technical information.[10] The question of the suitability of the program's design

---

[7] Office of the Undersecretary of Defense (Acquisition, Technology and Logistics), para 4.3.8 and para 4.3.9, 2002.

[8] The program and its antecedents have been in existence since 1961.

[9] Analysis at the level of individual IEPs may be problematic because individual programs may be too sensitive to personalities and similar factors, so the Air Force may prefer to treat IEPs in aggregate.

[10] U.S.C. Title 10, §2358, Chapter 139, and DoDI 2015.4 (Office of the Under Secretary of Defense (Acquisition, Technology and Logistics), 2002.

and theory, therefore, hinges on whether the individual IEPs, in aggregate, lead to the outcomes anticipated.

Step one in answering the question is to task the appropriate organizations and individuals for help. Taskings might include individual IEP agreement managers, laboratory directors in whose facilities the exchanges take place, individual IEP participants who might come from within the extended RDT&E community, and the Defense RDT&E IEP program management staff.

The second step, the test for logical consistency, involves identifying the assumptions about causality in the design and theory of the program and testing them against the available empirical data. The key assumptions can be identified through content analysis of the enabling legislation or Air Force documents describing the program and its expected benefits to the United States. It is worth noting that logical consistency is not subject to majority views; consensus among staff members does not guarantee it. Therefore, we must explicitly test the key assumptions that underpin the program's design and theory, and these are:

- A_1: that reciprocal exchanges produce additional technical cooperation among the participants
- A_2: that reciprocal exchanges lead to multinational force compatibility
- A_3: that reciprocal exchanges promote equitable access to new scientific and technical information.

Step three is to gather relevant data on the program. These might include individual IEP reports, individual IEP agreements, assessments of partner military capabilities, and copies of the actual materials shared during exchange activities.

Step four is the empirical test itself. It amounts to a counting exercise across time (perhaps over ten years) and across individual IEPs to test our assumptions A_1 through A_3. A_1 is confirmed if data show growth in technical cooperation (e.g., intensified frequency of meetings, larger numbers of participants, growth in the number of topics discussed). To ascertain whether growth occurred or not, we may have to count subsequent agreements on technical cooperation or numbers of exchange visits to see whether the trend points to growth, decline, or steady-state relations. A_2 is confirmed if data show an increase in multinational military capability. Here, the metrics might be changes in the size, robustness, and survivability of the partner forces, or increase in their expeditionary and power-projection capabilities, or perhaps increased growth in their interoperability with U.S. forces. A_3 is confirmed if data reveal a balanced exchange, measured perhaps by the number of documents exchanged, or by comparing the diversity in the number of topics covered by each party, or by measuring similar levels of scientific-technical complexity.

If all three key assumptions are confirmed, the design and theory of the IEPs can be said to be sound. If any one of the assumptions is disconfirmed, this indicates a flaw in the design and theory of the program that must be examined further to understand exactly what the disconnect is. Of course, because individual assumptions can fail independently of the others, this fact can help the Air Force formulate its overall recommendations about the program, by identifying those elements of program design and theory that are still sound (and thus producing expected results) from those that are not.

The fifth step is to assess the program's design and theory. Doing so involves pulling the threads together from the time-series data on IEPs with the test of key assumptions to arrive at conclusions about the overall suitability of the program's design and theory—that is, does it, in aggregate, produce the expected results? Then, depending on our confidence that the sample size (i.e., number of individual IEPs across the years) is sufficient to conclude that the IEPs reflect the suitability of design and theory of the RDT&E IEP generally, we can formulate a recommendation, once the validation and integration steps in our process run their course.

Validation and integration, steps six and seven, respectively, should closely resemble the same steps in our first example, so there is little to say about them specifically. The Air Force might involve the IG in the validation function given that office's familiarity with the program's operations and periodic inspections there. The SAF/IA might be the integrator for the results.

The final steps, formulating the recommendation and staffing it, would mirror the process described in the first example, but it may be worthwhile to describe in more detail some of the considerations for formulating the recommendation. In considering the recommendation that the Air Force might ultimately forward regarding the design and theory of the RDT&E IEP, the airmen working the issue should consider that the degree of logical consistency rests on the number of key assumptions that they have been able to identify in the instructions and literature describing the program. Thus, the more assumptions (i.e., expectations of cause and effect) the Air Force can identify, the better, because the more assumptions there are, the easier it becomes to identify specific failures in terms of cause-effect links. Added specificity in this regard means that the Air Force's ultimate recommendation can be highly nuanced.

Bibliography

Documents

Air Force Materiel Command, "Foreign Military Sales Resources," Air Force Materiel Command Instruction 16-101, undated.

Air University Instruction 16-102, "International Programs," May 14, 2008. As of October 13, 2009:
http://www.au.af.mil/msd/pubs/aui/aui16-102.pdf

Baldwin, Laura H., Frank Camm, and Nancy Y. Moore, *Strategic Sourcing: Measuring and Managing Performance*, Santa Monica, Calif.: RAND Corporation, DB-287-AF, 2000. As of April 30, 2009:
http://www.rand.org/pubs/documented_briefings/DB287/

Baldwin, Laura H., John A. Ausink, and Nancy Nicosia, *Air Force Service Procurement: Approaches for Measurement and Management*, Santa Monica, Calif.: RAND Corporation, MG-299-AF, 2005. As of April 30, 2009:
http://www.rand.org/pubs/monographs/MG299/

Berk, Richard A., and Peter H. Rossi, *Thinking About Program Evaluation*, Newbury Park, Calif.: Sage Publications, 1990.

Brown, Bernice B., *Delphi Process: A Methodology Used for the Elicitation of Opinions,* Santa Monica, Calif.: RAND Corporation, P-3925, 1968. As of October 23, 2009:
http://www.rand.org/pubs/papers/P3925/

Bush, President George W., *National Strategy for Combating Terrorism,* Washington, D.C., February 2003.

Chairman of the Joint Chiefs of Staff, *Joint Training Manual for the Armed Forces of the United States*, Manual 3500.03, undated-a.

———, *Assessment Program,* Instruction 3150.05, undated-b.

———, *Joint Lessons Learned Program,* Instruction 3150.25, undated-c.

————, *Implementation of a 2-Year Planning, Programming, Budgeting, and Execution Process,* Management Initiative Decision 913, May 22, 2003.

————, Joint Capabilities Integration and Development System, Instruction 3170.01E, May 11, 2005.

Defense Institute of Security Assistance Management, *Online Green Book: The Management of Security,* undated. As of September 18, 2008:
http://www.disam.dsca.mil/pubs/DR/greenbook.htm

Defense Security Cooperation Agency, "Frequently Asked Questions," April 29, 2009.

Deputy Under Secretary of the Air Force for International Affairs, *Security Assistance Handbook,* November 17, 2000.

————, ed., "Air Force Security Assistance Resource Board Briefing," Washington, D.C., 2003.

Diernisse, Lisa, "Performance Metrics for Non-Mathematicians," *Contract Management Magazine,* Vol. 43, No. 6, June 2003, pp. 44–53.

Draper, David, James S. Hodges, Edward E. Leamer, Carl N. Morris, and Donald B. Rubin, *A Research Agenda for Assessment and Propagation of Model Uncertainty,* Santa Monica, Calif.: RAND Corporation, N-2683-RC, 1987. As of October 23, 2009:
http://www.rand.org/pubs/notes/N2683/

Eaton, Yvonne, "Distinguished Visitor Orientation Tour and Orientation Tour Program," *The DISAM Journal,* Fall 2003. As of August 25, 2008:
http://www.disam.dsca.mil/pubs/Indexes/v.26_1/Eaton.pdf

GlobalSecurity.org, "US Military Exercises," undated. As of September 18, 2008:
http://www.globalsecurity.org/military/ops/ex.htm

Grimes, Major Derek I., Major John Rawcliffe, and Captain Jeannine Smith, eds., *2006 Operational Law Handbook,* Judge Advocate General's Corps, 2006. As of September 19, 2007:
https://www.mfp.usmc.mil/TeamApp/SJA/Topics/20051028095223/OPLAW%20HB%20Chapter%2011,%20Fiscal%20Law.pdf

Hatry, Harry P., *Performance Measurement: Getting Results,* 2nd ed., Washington, D.C.: Urban Institute Press, 2007.

Hoehn, Andrew R., Adam Grissom, David Ochmanek, David A. Shlapak, and Alan J. Vick, *A New Division of Labor: Meeting America's Security Challenges Beyond Iraq*, Santa Monica, Calif.: RAND Corporation, MG-499-AF, 2007. As of November 10, 2008:
http://www.rand.org/pubs/monographs/MG499/

Hoffman, Tim, "Guidance for the Employment of the Force," paper presented at the ODASD Partnership Strategy Worldwide Joint Training and Scheduling Conference, Fort Leavenworth, Kan., September 17–21, 2007.

Lemkin, Bruce, "International Relationships: Critical Enablers for Expeditionary Air and Space Operations," *The DISAM Journal*, Vol. 28, No. 1, Fall 2005.

Marquis, Jefferson P., Richard E. Darilek, Jasen J. Castillo, Cathryn Quantic Thurston, Anny Wong, Cynthia Huger, Andrea Mejia, Jennifer D.P. Moroney, Brian Nichiporuk, and Brett Steele, *Assessing the Value of U.S. Army International Activities*, Santa Monica, Calif.: RAND Corporation, MG-329-A, 2006. As of February 12, 2008:
http://www.rand.org/pubs/monographs/MG329/.

Martin, Kenneth, W., "Legislation for Fiscal Year 2008," *The DISAM Journal*, Vol. 30, No. 2, June 2008, pp. 1–91. As of September 28, 2008:
http://www.disam.dsca.mil/pubs/Indexes/Vol%2030_2/Journal%20%2030-2.pdf

Moroney, Jennifer D.P., Adam Grissom, and Jefferson P. Marquis, *A Capabilities-Based Strategy for Army Security Cooperation*, MG-563-A, Santa Monica, Calif.: RAND Corporation, 2007. As of November 10, 2008:
http://www.rand.org/pubs/monographs/MG563/

Moroney, Jennifer D.P., Nancy E. Blacker, Renee Buhr, James McFadden, Cathryn Quantic Thurston, and Anny Wong, *Building Partner Capabilities for Coalition Operations*, MG-635-A, Santa Monica, Calif.: RAND Corporation, 2007. As of November 10, 2008:
http://www.rand.org/pubs/monographs/MG635/

Moroney, Jennifer D.P., Kim Cragin, Eric Gons, Beth Grill, John E. Peters, and Rachel M. Swanger, *International Cooperation with Partner Air Forces,* MG-790-AF, Santa Monica, Calif.: RAND Corporation, 2009. As of November 3, 2009:
http://www.rand.org/pubs/monographs/MG790/

National Defense Strategy of the United States, March 2005.

National Military Strategic Plan—War on Terrorism, 2006.

National Military Strategy of the United States, 2004.

National Security Strategy of the United States, March 2006.

Office of Air Force International Affairs Strategic Plan, 2005.

Office of the Secretary of Defense, *Security Cooperation Guidance*, 2006.

————, *Guidance for Employment of the Force,* 2008.

Office of the Under Secretary of Defense (Acquisition, Technology and Logistics), DoDI 2015.4, February 7, 2002.

Paul, Christopher, Harry J. Thie, Elaine Reardon, Deanna Weber Prine, and Laurence Smallman, *Implementing and Evaluating an Innovative Approach to Simulation Training Acquisitions,* Santa Monica, Calif.: RAND Corporation, MG-442-OSD, 2006. As of April 30, 2009: http://www.rand.org/pubs/monographs/MG442/

Phillips, W. Darrell, "Use of Operation and Maintenance Funds During Deployments," *Armed Forces Controller,* Fall 2006, pp. 27–31.

Rossi, Peter H., Mark W. Lipsey, and Howard E. Freeman, *Evaluation: A Systematic Approach,* 7th ed., Thousand Oaks, Calif.: Sage Publications, 2004.

Secretary of the Air Force/International Affairs, *Strategic Plan 2008.*

U.S. Air Force, *Joint Security Assistance Training,* Air Force Joint Instruction 16-105, undated-a.

————, *Readiness Exercises and After-Action Reporting Program,* Air Force Instruction 10-204, undated-b.

————, "Operations Support International Affairs," Air Force Policy Directive 16-1, August 16, 1993.

————, *Dedicated Foreign Military Sales Training Programs,* Air Force Instruction 65-607, 1997a.

————, *Operations Support: Latin American Cooperation Fund,* Air Force Instruction 16-102, May 1, 1997b.

————, *Training Development, Delivery, and Evaluation,* Air Force Instruction 36-2201, Vol. 1, 2002.

————, *International Affairs and Security Assistance Management,* Air Force Manual 16-101, 2003a.

————, *US Air Force Participation in International Armaments Cooperation (IAC),* Air Force Instruction 16-110, November 4, 2003b. As of September 16, 2008: http://www.e-publishing.af.mil/shared/media/epubs/AFI16-110.pdf

————, *Air Force Basic Doctrine,* Air Force Doctrine Document 1, November 17, 2003c.

————, Manpower and Organization, *Headquarters United States Air Force, Organization and Functions,* Air Force Pamphlet 38-102, January 1, 2004a.

————, *Inspector General Activities,* Air Force Instruction 90-201, November 22, 2004b.

————, Official Representation Funds—Guidance and Procedures, Air Force Instruction 65-603, February 17, 2004c.

————, *Military Personnel Exchange Program (MPEP)*, Air Force Instruction 16-107, 2006a. As of April 29, 2009: http://www.e-publishing.af.mil/

————, Office of the Secretary of the Air Force for International Affairs, *Air Force Security Cooperation Strategy*, September 11, 2006b.

————, *Control and Documentation of Air Force Programs*, Air Force Instruction 16-501, 2006d.

————, *Managers' Internal Control Program Procedures*, Air Force Instruction 65-201, 2006e.

————, "Air Force Studies and Analyses, Assessments, and Learned," Headquarters Air Force Mission Directive 1-58, 2007.

"U.S. Air Force Global Partnerships Strategy: Building Partnership Capability and Capacity for the 21st Century," draft, 2008.

U.S.C. Title 10, Chapter 905, Aviation Leadership Program, January 8, 2008.

U.S.C. Title 22, Foreign Relations and Intercourse, Sec. 2763, Credit Sales, 2003.

U.S. Department of Defense, *Department of Defense Dictionary of Military and Associated Terms*, Joint Publication 1-02, undated-a.

————, "Department of Defense Fiscal Year (FY) 2003 Budget Estimates and Justification," undated-b. As of September 15, 2008: http://www.defenselink.mil/comptroller/defbudget/fy2003/budget_justification/pdfs/03_RDT_and_E/rdte_vol3.pdf

————, "Security Assistance Policy and Procedures," undated-c.

————, *Security Assistance Management Manual*, Department of Defense Directive 5105.38-M, Chapter 10, October 3, 2003. As of August 15, 2009: http://www.dsca.mil/SAMM/

————, "Visits and Assignments of Foreign Nationals," DoD Directive 5230.20, 2005a. As of October 13, 2009: http://www.dtic.mil/whs/directives/corres/html/523020.htm

————, Office of the Inspector General, *Joint Warfighting and Readiness, DoD Execution of the Warsaw Initiative Program*, D-2005-085, July 1, 2005b.

————, *Quadrennial Defense Review Report*, February 6, 2006a. As of February 12, 2008: http://www.dod.mil/pubs/pdfs/QDR20060203.pdf

———, *Building Partnership Capacity Roadmap*, Washington, D.C., September 2006b.

———, Office of the Under Secretary of Defense for Acquisition, Technology and Logistics, *International Armaments Cooperation Handbook, 4th ed.*, November 2006c.

———, *Security Assistance Management Manual*, DoD 5105.38-M, 2007. As of April 29, 2009:
http://www.dsca.mil/SAMM

———, Financial Management Regulation 7000.14-R, 2008.

U.S. Department of State, *Foreign Military Training Reports,* undated. As of May 12, 2009:
http://www.state.gov/t/pm/rls/rpt/fmtrpt/

———, "Foreign Military Training: Joint Report to Congress, Fiscal Years 2006 and 2007," Bureau of Political-Military Affairs, August 2007. As of September 19, 2008:
http://www.state.gov/t/pm/rls/rpt/fmtrpt/2007/92071.htm

U.S. Government Accountability Office, *Government Auditing Standards, Revision,* GAO-07-731G, Washington, D.C., July 27, 2007a.

———, "Section 1206 Security Assistance Program: Findings on Criteria, Coordination, and Implementation," GAO-07-416R, February 28, 2007b. As of September 19, 2008:
http://www.gao.gov/docsearch/abstract.php?rptno=GAO-07-416R

Vick, Alan, Adam Grissom, William Rosenau, Beth Grill, and Karl P. Mueller, *Air Power in the New Counterinsurgency Era: The Strategic Importance of USAF Advisory and Assistance Missions*, Santa Monica, Calif.: RAND Corporation, MG-509-AF, 2006. As of November 10, 2008:
http://www.rand.org/pubs/monographs/MG509/

Ward, General William, "The USEUCOM Strategic Effectiveness Process," *Joint Forces Quarterly*, Issue 44, 1st Quarter 2007.

The White House, *National Security Strategy of the United States of America,* Washington, D.C., September 2002.

Focused Discussions

6 Air Force Special Operations Squadron

Air Education and Training Command, International Affairs

Air Force Security Assistance Center

Air Force Security Assistance Training Squadron

Defense Security Cooperation Agency

Headquarters Air Force/A3/5

Inter-American Air Force Academy

Joint Staff J-5

National Guard Bureau, International Affairs

Office of the Deputy Under Secretary of the Air Force for International Affairs

Office of the Secretary of Defense for Policy, Partnership Strategy

Office of the Secretary of Defense for Policy, Policy Planning

U.S. Air Force Central Command, A5

U.S. Air Force European Command, A5

U.S. Air Force Pacific Command, A5

U.S. Air Force Southern Command, A5

U.S. Army Security Assistance Command

U.S. Army Security Assistance Training Management Organization

U.S. Central Command, J5

U.S. European Command, J5

U.S. Marine Corps (Security Cooperation Office, Quantico Marine Corps Base)

U.S. Pacific Command, J56